A
THOUSAND
DISTANT
SHORES

A
THOUSAND
DISTANT
SHORES

BUCK TURNER

PAGE
—&—
VINE

Page & Vine
An Imprint of Meredith Wild LLC

Paperback ISBN: 978-1-964264-09-7

To Leon,
without whom none of this would be possible.

PROLOGUE

*To be a lighthouse, you must be strong enough to resist every
kind of storm, to every kind of loneliness and you must have a
powerful light inside you!*
—Mehmet Murat Ildan

October 1993

She stands alone.

Staring out at the angry Atlantic, she watches a storm
brewing on the horizon, the thick clouds gathering strength and
momentum as they roll closer to the shore. Below her, the sea
roils and churns, the wind tangles her hair into knots. Despite
the ominous scene, she is entranced by the dark, brooding
expanse of water, its surface a tempestuous dance of swirling
whirlpools and white-capped waves.

In the distance, the lighthouse pulses steadily, an
unwavering beacon fighting against the encroaching darkness.
As the storm draws nearer, the lighthouse's beam becomes
increasingly frantic, spinning and slicing through the churning
sea as if seeking out some unseen threat lurking beneath its
surface.

Her fingers graze over the metal railing, the chill sinking
into her skin. She can taste the salt on her lips and feel the
sting of the ocean as the spray hits her face. A sudden flash

3

of lightning splits the sky, followed almost immediately by a guttural roar of thunder.

She turns away, and her thoughts drift to the New York Times article she read earlier that morning. She can still picture the headline, stark black letters burned into her mind— "TRAILBLAZING ASTRONOMER RECEIVES NASA'S HIGHEST HONOR." Her grip tightens around the iron railing as she contemplates the story of Dr. Elizabeth Spencer-Bennett—the same woman who was once her teenage rival. She pulls her sweater tighter around her shoulders, a sudden chill rippling through her that has little to do with the impending storm. Memories of summers long ago flood back, vivid and visceral. The long nights spent praying he would choose her instead of Ellie, and the bitter taste of disappointment that lingered when he did not. In the end, it was always Ellie who captured his attention, her brilliant mind and stunning beauty drawing him in like a moth to a flame.

How naïve she had been back then, to think that her bond with Jack could have weathered a storm like Ellie.

A gust of wind whips the hair across her face, pulling her from her musing. The storm is upon her, the rumble of thunder echoing across the vast expanse. She knows she should head inside, seek shelter from the approaching squall. But something keeps her rooted to the spot. Maybe it's the allure of the storm, the raw power of nature unleashed. Or perhaps it's the twisted sense of kinship she feels with the roiling waves. Regardless, she braces herself and leans into the wind, ready to face whatever onslaught the storm will bring.

PART 1

CHAPTER 1

October 1993

Sunday

The sound of the doorbell echoed through the cavernous beachside mansion. Tearing my gaze away from the pages of my favorite novel, I looked up, my eyes narrowing at the interruption.

Is it time already? I glanced at the clock on the antique mahogany sideboard, its hands pointing at a quarter past four. With a sigh, I rose and eased toward the hallway, my bones creaking like the old wooden steps leading to the lighthouse in the distance. Guests were rare these days, but that didn't diminish the stir of excitement that visitors brought. For decades, this mansion had been a hub of social activity, its rooms often filled with the laughter and chatter of Kitty Hawk's political and social elite. The memories of those days clung to the high-ceilinged rooms like the scent of old perfume, bringing with them a touch of melancholy.

But today was different. As I approached the grand oak door, there was a spark of anticipation in the air, a tingle of unfamiliarity that promised a break from the monotony of my quiet life.

Through the frosted glass, I spotted a silhouette—a lean

figure, distinctly feminine, draped in a coat that danced around her ankles. My heart caught in my chest. When I agreed to have my biography written, I hadn't expected to feel so nervous, so naked. And yet here I was, as vulnerable as a peach without its protective skin. With one last glance back toward the sanctity of my library, I took a deep breath, knowing that once I opened the door, there was no going back.

Under the overhang, sheltering from the pouring rain, stood Diane Montgomery. She was an attractive young woman, in an obvious sort of way—long dark hair teased by the wind, a tailored emerald green pea coat that flattered her frame, and eyes of sapphire that sparkled with intelligence. Beneath her arm, she carried a brown leather satchel, no doubt filled with notebooks, pens, and perhaps even a tape recorder. All tools of the trade. Diane was a twenty-eight-year-old single mother and aspiring writer, employed as an investigative journalist for the Stanly News & Press in Albemarle, a suburb of Charlotte. She had come to spend the week with me, to chronicle my life in a book that she had been eager to write.

Initially, I had been skeptical. Who would want to read the story of a woman past her prime marooned in an oversized beach house? But the more I pondered, the more I realized that my life had been anything but ordinary. From my humble beginnings as a poor country girl to becoming a judge, my journey had been filled with trials and triumphs. Yet, it was the personal life behind the public persona that Diane wanted to unravel, those intimate chapters shrouded by the fog of time. In her letter, she stated that I had been an inspiration to her, a beacon of hope in a world where women often felt overshadowed and underappreciated. With the promise of respect and sincerity, she asked for my consent to share my story with the world. I agreed, albeit with a touch of apprehension.

As soon as I opened the door, Diane smiled and extended a hand. Her grip was firm, her manicured nails painted a ruby red. "Good afternoon, Your Honor," she said, her voice rich and warm like a freshly brewed cup of coffee. "It's a pleasure to finally meet you in person."

"Likewise. Won't you come in? And please, call me Sara."

Diane stepped into the foyer, the heels of her boots clicking on the polished marble. "What a beautiful home you have, Sara," she said, taking a moment to admire the grand staircase and ornate chandelier that hung in the center of the room.

"Thank you." I watched her closely, trying to discern whether the admiration in her voice was genuine or just a practiced courtesy of her profession. However, her eyes, lively and expressive, seemed to drink in the details with genuine interest. "It's seen many a stormy day," I added, gesturing toward the tall bay windows flanking the room that framed the inclement weather outside.

Diane followed my gaze to the gray clouds that churned in the sky, the rivulets of rain that slipped down the windowpane. "I can only imagine."

"Please, let me take your coat."

She shrugged it off with a grateful smile, revealing a tailored white blouse tucked into a maroon pencil skirt beneath. "Thank you. This weather is quite something, isn't it?"

I took her coat and hung it in the closet next to the entrance. "Indeed. Unpredictable, like most things in life." I led her into the library, where a fire crackled in the hearth. The room was a delightfully eclectic blend of old-world charm and contemporary style. It boasted high ceilings with intricate moldings, elegant wooden paneling, grand windows draped in luxurious maroon velvet curtains, and walls adorned with an impressive collection of books and exquisite artwork. The warm glow of the fire bathed the room in a warm ambiance, making it a sanctuary against the gloomy weather outside.

Diane's eyes roamed across the room, taking in the collection of first-edition books and the rich details of each painting. "Marvelous. Simply marvelous." Her sharp gaze landed on a painting, a somber piece of a girl seemingly trying to climb up a hill. "This is Christina's World, is it not?"

"I'm impressed. It belonged to my late husband. He had such a keen eye for art."

"And what about you? Do you share his passion?"

I poured two glasses of iced tea from an ornate silver pitcher and handed one to Diane. "I appreciate art, but my passion lies elsewhere." I gestured toward the towering bookcase that lined the far wall. "I find the written word to be the most expressive form of art."

Diane took a moment to appreciate the vast array of literature before her. Bound volumes of classic works, historical recounts, contemporary novels, and even poetry collections filled the shelves from floor to ceiling. They were organized not by author or title, but color—a rainbow of spines that brought vibrancy to the room. "That's quite a collection."

"Would you believe this isn't half of it?"

Her eyes widened in surprise. "You must be quite the reader. Do you have a favorite?"

"It's like asking a mother to pick a favorite child. But if I had to choose one, it would be The Great Gatsby. It's a tale of love, deception, and the façade of the American Dream. I find something new each time I read it."

Diane nodded as she sipped her tea. "It's been ages since

I read that one. Probably not since high school English class."

"If you enjoy reading, you're welcome to any book you like during your stay. Speaking of which, we took the liberty of preparing the cottage for you. I hope that's okay?"

"We?"

"Judy and I. She's one of my dearest friends and has been staying with me since my husband passed away. A recent widow herself, she and I have become each other's support system."

"I'm sorry for your losses. It's good to have someone to lean on during tough times."

"Yes, it is," I said, fighting a lump in my throat. "And might I add, it's also good to have a distraction. Like your visit. I've been looking forward to this for quite some time."

"I'm glad to hear you say that," she replied. "I have been, too. Believe it or not, this is my first trip to the Outer Banks."

"Well, you've picked the perfect time to visit," I said gesturing toward the window where the rain continued to fall in sheets. "Once this storm passes, you'll see how the fall brings out the true beauty of these shores."

"Speaking of beautiful, is that the cottage you were telling me about?" She moved over to the window, her gaze seeking out the small structure nestled at the edge of the dunes.

"That's it. My little home away from home. You'll have plenty of peace and quiet there while you work. Once this storm passes, I'll be happy to show it to you."

"That's very kind of you. Thank you."

"Of course."

Diane nodded appreciatively, her eyes taking one last sweep of the grand library before returning to me. "Tell me, was it difficult transitioning from a humble life to...this?"

I chuckled, reflecting on my journey. "Difficult? No, I

wouldn't say it was difficult. A little overwhelming, especially at the beginning, but I like to think that I took to it like a duck to water." I led Diane toward a plush seating area near the grand fireplace. I settled onto a tufted velvet chair while she claimed the seat opposite me on a matching chaise, crossing one leg over the other. Her eyes twinkled with intrigue as she set her tea on a walnut coffee table and pulled a notepad from her satchel.

"Thanks again for agreeing to do this. When you responded to my letter, I must admit, I was a bit surprised, especially given your reputation for reticence. If you don't mind me asking, is there a particular reason you want to do this now?"

"For starters, my career has afforded me the luxury of solitude, the privilege of distance. For years, I've watched people form assumptions about me, my life, this house...and I've let them. I've realized, though, that silence can be just as much a lie as any spoken words. If people are going to talk, I want them to have the right information. Now that I'm retired, I feel it's time for me to write my own narrative. The true version of my story, not the fragmented pieces that have been stitched together by intrigued outsiders. Ultimately, I feel like this is my chance to do what I do best—to plead my case and show the rest of the world that I'm not the heartless woman they think I am."

Diane nodded, her fingers tapping against the spine of her notepad. "That's incredibly brave. But why me? Out of all the wonderful and accomplished writers you could have chosen, why invite me, a mere novice, into your world?"

The question hung in the air between us like a lingering mist. I leaned back in my chair, steepling my fingers. "It's true, I've been approached by numerous writers—some famous, some not, all clamoring for the golden ticket into my world. But your letter... It touched me. It was genuine and heartfelt.

But more than that, I wanted the truth to be told, not an embellished version designed to attract attention. You don't know this, but I've tracked your career for quite some time. I've read your articles, admired your investigative prowess, and more importantly, respected your integrity. You have a rare gift for listening to the undercurrents, the hidden truth between the lines. There was one article in particular, 'The Man Behind the Mask,' that resonated with me deeply. You wrote, 'True power does not come from wealth or status, but from authenticity, from the courage to reveal oneself fully and fearlessly to the world.' It was one of the few times I felt someone understood what it means to be in this position. You didn't just focus on the superficial, the glamour, and the indulgence. You peered beneath the surface, into the abyss where the real person dwells. That's why you're here, Diane. I believe you're capable of telling my story with that same integrity."

A slow smile spread across her face. It was clear that my words had hit their mark. "I'm flattered. And I promise you I'll do my best to capture your truth." She took a sip of tea before going on. "You know, it's not every day that I have the pleasure of talking with a woman of your caliber. Typically, I find myself in the company of local businessmen or politicians, but never a judge, let alone a female one."

I laughed, finding it amusing that she thought my life so extraordinary. "I suppose it's because we judges are usually behind the bench, not in front of a reporter's pen. But I think it's important to share our stories as well. And I'm honored to be your first."

"Speaking of being honored." Diane's expression turned serious as she uncapped her pen. "How does it feel to be only the second female Supreme Court Justice in the state's history?"

"It's overwhelming, to be honest. When I started my law career, women were still a rarity in the field. To have risen to where I am now, it feels like I've scaled a mountain. But it's not just about me. It's about every young girl out there who needs the courage to be whatever she wants to be, even in a predominantly male industry. It's also proof that no matter where you come from or what your circumstances are, you can rise above them and achieve great things."

Diane's pen danced across the paper as she scribbled my words. "I like that...that spirit of empowerment. Has that always been a driving force in your life?"

"Not always. My early years were heavily influenced by the notion that my life should follow a traditional path—marry well, have children, be content with a quiet, domestic life. It was only when I finally left my small town that my worldview began to expand."

"And is that when you realized you wanted to have a career in law, or have you always known?"

I laughed, recalling my youthful dreams. "Actually, I did have early aspiration of being a lawyer, but I was too shy to even dream of standing before a courtroom. So I dismissed it as an impossible dream and decided to be a teacher instead. In fact, I graduated with a mathematics degree from the University of Tennessee with the intention of doing just that. For a while, I even toyed with the notion of becoming a college professor. It wasn't until years later that I was given a second chance to follow my original dream."

Diane's pen paused and she looked up. "And what led you on that path? There must have been a turning point, yes?"

I allowed my mind to journey along the threads of my memory. "Yes, indeed there was. But perhaps we should save that for later. I don't want to spoil the plot. We're only in chapter one, after all."

"Fair enough," Diane said, her professional demeanor faltering for the briefest of moments, replaced by a flicker of unguarded curiosity. She clicked her pen, collecting herself. "Just so you know, I typically like to split my interviews into three parts—past, present, and future. I like to start with the journey that has brought you here, then delve into what you're currently engaged in, and finally get a glimpse of where you might be headed. How does that sound?"

"Sounds like a fair approach. And I promise to tell the truth, the whole truth, and nothing but the truth, so help me God," I said, working in some lawyer humor.

Diane chuckled and glanced at her wristwatch. "We probably should wait until tomorrow to really dig into your past, but I'd like to ask a few preliminary questions, you know, to break the ice. Are you up for that?"

"Fire away."

She pulled out the recorder and flipped the switch, the red light flickering on. "Let's start with your early years. Tell me about the town you grew up in. What was it like?"

I glanced at the flames in the fireplace, my mind traveling back to the days of my childhood. "I was born in a little town called Sims Chapel, the only child of a single mother that loved me more than life itself. It was a place where everyone knew each other's name, and secrets could hardly be kept secret. Nestled between the Smoky Mountains and a river that kissed the edges of town, Sims Chapel was as charming as any small town could be."

"It sounds like a lovely place."

"Oh, it was. Unlike the mansion we now sit in, my childhood

home was neither fancy nor glamorous. But it sat atop a rolling hill with a view of the mountains that would take your breath away. In the winter, when the trees were bare, you could see all the way down to the river." I paused, feeling the weight of years that had passed, the memories layered like paint on an old wall. "Before the Tennessee Valley Authority came in and dammed up the river, I used to swim and play in its cool waters. Until I got old enough to swim properly, my mother would sit on the bank, humming to herself while mending clothes.

"It sounds as if your mother played a significant role in your upbringing," Diane interjected. "Tell me more about her."

I nodded, absorbed in the memories. "My daddy died before I was born, so Mother was everything to me. A guiding light, a pillar of strength. She taught me kindness and respect, showed me the pain of hard work and the joy its fruits could bring. She was a seamstress, working long hours to keep food on the table and clothes on my back. She used to say that she sewed pieces of her heart into everything she made."

"I like that. What about your friends? Did you have many?"

"Most of the kids my age lived in Dandridge, which was up the river a bit, but there were a few in Sims Chapel. Yvonne Tidwell and Connie Barnes were both close friends of mine. But my best friend was a boy named Jack Bennett. He and I were two peas in a pod, inseparable from the day we met. Jack was the adventurous type, always up for just about anything, constantly dragging me into the woods or down to the river on one of his exploits."

"So you were a tomboy?"

"Oh yes, very much so. I was climbing trees and scraping my knees before I could read and write. Jack and I would spend the day exploring the woods, fishing down by the river, or playing pretend in the old barn at the back of his family's property. Mother was forever washing dirt out of my clothes and scolding me for coming home past sundown. But she was always there, waiting on the porch with a warm smile and a hot meal."

Diane chuckled softly. "So is it safe to say that you and Jack were partners in crime?"

"I reckon we were. We were mischievous, no doubt about it. At least I was. I had this knack for finding trouble, you see, and Jack had a knack for getting us out of it. We'd explore the land together, looking for arrowheads and old artifacts, or sneak down to the creek and catch crawfish with our bare hands. Jack had a wild, free spirit about him, like the wind in the trees. It was infectious...made me want to follow him on whatever crazy adventure he had planned out for that day."

"And did your mother know about your exploits?"

"Oh, she knew about them all right." A smile pulled at the corners of my mouth. "I think she wanted me to be more like the other girls—quiet, gentle, and clean. But she also understood my need for adventure and freedom. She knew I wouldn't be content with sewing circles and tea parties. No, I needed the open air, the feel of the dirt under my feet and the freedom of the wild. As long as I got good grades and was home in time for dinner, she was content. At least she pretended to be."

Diane's eyebrows went up a notch at that, her pen racing across the page again. "It's clear your mother played a significant role in your life, but what about your friend, Jack. Was he influential as well?"

I paused for a moment, my gaze cast down, to remember a face that time had begun to blur. "Yes, Jack was...is...a huge part of who I am."

Before I knew it, an hour had passed. Diane had a way of making the minutes vanish, one question melting into another with seamless grace.

"Thank you for being so candid with me this afternoon," Diane said as she put away her things. "We're off to a good start."

"My pleasure," I said as I stood and made my way to the window. Outside, the rain had stopped, and the first rays of sunlight were beginning to pierce through the thinning clouds. "See, what did I tell you. Just look at that view."

"Gorgeous," Diane replied, her eyes wide as she joined me by the window. "Does this mean we can see the cottage now?"

"Absolutely," I said, motioning her toward the door. "Follow me."

CHAPTER 2

We walked to the edge of the lawn, where the damp manicured grass met the sandy path leading to the beach. Down below, the cottage stood among the dunes and palm trees, its weather-beaten shingles faded to a soft grey under the relentless kiss of sea spray and sun. The windows were half-hidden by wild roses that had climbed up the trellis, their thorny stems intertwining with the lattice in a tenacious display of nature's will.

As we made our way down the sandy path, the crunch of damp sand and hollow shells bounced off the nearby dunes, sending whispers across the landscape. The salty breeze tugged at my clothes, imbuing them with that distinct, briny scent of the sea. With the day waning, long shadows stretched out, dancing like silent phantoms against the sand.

"No one lives here?" Diane asked as we neared the cottage.

"Not at the moment," I said, opening the small gate for her. "But I'm thinking of taking on a tenant, someone who can appreciate the beauty of this place as much as I do." We moved ahead. "This area used to be nothing but sand and scrub brush until my husband had it cleared. He built the cottage for me shortly after we were married... Said if I was to be a proper lawyer, I needed an escape—a sanctuary away from the world, where I could think and work in peace."

"It sounds like he was a considerate man."

"Yes, he was. Full of fire and compassion. He loved this

place. But he loved me even more. He had a deep understanding of the world and of people. He could see what others couldn't and had this uncanny ability to make dreams come true. I miss him dearly."

We stepped onto the wooden porch of the cottage, our footsteps muted by the aged planks.

"I can't get over this place," Diane said as she turned and looked out at the ocean. "It's so beautiful. Do you spend a lot of time out here?"

"When I was younger, I did. But these days, I mostly keep to the house."

"So it just sits empty? What a shame."

We approached the weather-beaten door. Peeling paint revealed layers of colors reflecting my changing tastes over the years. The brass doorknob was speckled with patches of green, evidence of the many seasons it had survived. The old door creaked open at my touch, revealing a light and airy interior. The cottage consisted of two large rooms, divided by a worn brick archway. One room was a combination of living area and kitchen, with a small bathroom tucked off to the side. A loft area above held an oversized king bed, complete with a white canopy that fluttered gently in the breeze from the open window. There was a rustic charm to it, a simplicity that belied its age and history. The wooden floorboards were worn smooth from years of use, their grain visible beneath the layers of lacquer. The walls were adorned with a smattering of old nautical maps and framed black and white photographs.

The kitchen was modest, with a fridge, stove, and well-worn wooden counters. A set of mismatched china filled the open shelves, alongside jars full of home-canned fruit preserves and pickles. A kettle sat on the stove, and next to it, two cups with tea bags waiting to be steeped. In the living area, a soft wool rug lay before a stone fireplace, the mantel adorned with seashells and small driftwood sculptures. An overstuffed armchair and a matching sofa, both upholstered in faded floral fabric, faced the hearth. And a small writing desk sat against the opposite wall beneath a window that overlooked the sea.

A sense of tranquility pervaded the room, as if time had stopped within its aged walls. It was a place where one could spend countless hours reading, writing, or simply contemplating the mysteries of life.

"Wow," Diane said, her eyes wide as she took in the place. "This is...amazing. Like something out of a storybook."

I smiled, pleased by her reaction. "Yes, it certainly feels that way sometimes. I've spent many an afternoon here, lost in the pages of a novel, the outside world forgotten."

"Are these the books you were telling me about?" She pointed at the packed bookshelves that lined the far wall.

I nodded. "Each one has been a companion at some point. I began collecting books shortly after I moved to Kitty Hawk, and the collection has grown ever since. They've always been my escape."

Diane moved further into the room, tracing her hand along the back of the sofa, her fingers lingering on the faded blooms woven into the fabric. Watching her explore, I was reminded of the first time I had stepped into this cottage, swept up in its charm. I was happy then, more so than I'd ever been in my life. Now, seeing her enchantment with the place, I felt that sense of joy returning.

"I envy whoever ends up staying here." She paused, her attention drawn to the writing desk. "Oh, the stories longing to be written in this space. It's inspiring."

"I thought the same when I first walked into this room. Sadly, I've never been much of a writer."

"I've always dreamed of having a place like this...a place where I could sit and let my mind wander. I can't thank you enough for allowing me to stay here."

"It's my pleasure."

For a moment, she seemed lost in thought, her eyes distant and dreamy. Eventually, she turned back to me and said, "Believe it or not, I too lost my husband recently. His name was Kyle. Before he died, we had talked about finding a place on the ocean, where we could hear the call of the gulls and the whisper of the tide. We dreamed of raising our family there and spending our twilight years watching the sunsets and letting the sounds of the sea lull us to sleep." She paused and shook away the melancholy that seemed to have settled upon her. "But now, it's just me and my daughter, Cassie."

Caught off guard by her confession, I felt a sudden pang of empathy. "I'm terribly sorry for your loss. I didn't realize..."

"Thank you. It's been hard, but we're doing the best we can. One day at a time, right?"

"To have your dreams taken from you is a cruel thing."

"It's like a piece of you is ripped away, leaving a gaping hole that never quite heals." Eventually, she forced a small smile. "I'm sorry for unloading all that on you. It's just...this place reminds me so much of him and the dreams we once had."

"There's no need to apologize, dear. And if you'd rather stay in the house with me and Judy, you're more than welcome to do so."

"No, this is perfect. I think this is exactly where I need to be."

By the time we made our way back to the house, Judy was

waiting for us at the door. "You're just in time. Supper's almost ready."

"I hope you're hungry," I said as I led her inside. "I had Judy prepare a special dish of shrimp and grits for us. It's a local favorite."

Diane's eyes lit up. "Can't wait. But do you mind if I make a call before dinner? I want to check in with Cassie, make sure she's settled in at my aunt's."

"Of course." I showed her to the small study off the main hallway. "And take your time."

When Diane closed herself inside, I turned back down the hall, my thoughts drifting to the pieces of my life I had shared with her that afternoon. We had only begun to scratch the surface, but already I was feeling an unfamiliar vulnerability rise within me as memories, dusty and forgotten, awakened from their slumber.

CHAPTER 3

When Diane had finished her call, she joined me in the dining room for supper. Now that the storm was gone, the evening light filtered through the windows, tinting our faces in shades of apricot and honey.

"Smells delicious, Judy," I said as I topped off our glasses with sweet tea.

Judy poked her head in from the kitchen, a beaming smile on her face and a wooden spoon in hand. "Thank you. Supper is coming right up."

Diane watched in awe as our plates were served. She confessed that she wasn't much of a cook, and that many of her meals consisted of fast food and frozen dinners. "It's not that I don't care for good food, but the long hours spent at the newspaper rarely afford me the time to prepare something as grand as this. Plus, Cassie is happier with a box of chicken nuggets and apple slices than anything I can whip up."

Before we indulged ourselves in the feast before us, I blessed the food and the hands that prepared it. "May it nourish our bodies and our souls," I said, before adding, "Amen."

Finally, we dug in, the comforting sounds of cutlery scraping plates and contented sighs filling the room.

"I thought this afternoon went well," said Diane between bites. "Don't you?"

"Quite," I agreed, my fork hovering midway to my mouth.

"Which is a little surprising, considering it's been years since I've opened up about my past."

"I think it's good, you know, to open up. It has a healing effect, sort of like letting fresh air into a stuffy room."

There was a rustic charm to the moment—the fading grapefruit hues of the sunset streaming through the kitchen window, the warm aroma of Judy's cooking, and Diane's comforting presence.

"We all lug our past with us," Diane continued as she looked down at her half-eaten bowl. "It's like a shadow that follows us everywhere we go. But, like my mother used to tell me, it's up to us whether we let it weigh us down or if we adjust the straps and learn to carry it with grace."

"Your mother is a wise woman," I said, thinking how my past tended to lurk behind me, a silent specter ever-present in my life. "I suppose that's why I enjoy these quiet moments, in the comfort of family and friends. They've always provided an escape from the burdens that seek to claim my peace of mind. And you're right," I admitted, pushing around the remaining grits in my bowl. "The past is always there, and we do carry it with us, no matter how hard we try to leave it behind."

When supper was over, Diane and I went our separate ways, agreeing to resume our conversation over breakfast the next morning. After cleaning up, I wandered to the porch, drawn by the comforting blanket of twilight. I settled into the old wicker chair, my body yielding to its familiar contours, and it wasn't long before Judy joined me.

"So, is she what you expected?"

"Honestly? I can't say I really knew what to expect. She's certainly every bit as determined as I thought she'd be. And she's definitely got a wisdom about her, a sort of quiet strength that I admire. But there's something terribly sad about her as well, something that lingers in her eyes. She told me this afternoon that she recently lost her husband. And at her age... Can you believe it?"

"Sorrow knows no age," said Judy. "Of all people, you should know that."

"I know. It's just hard to see others go through the pain. Especially someone so young."

After a moment, Judy turned to me and said, "It's strange, isn't it? The three of us here together, at different stages of life, all widowed?"

"Yes, it is," I replied, staring out at the encroaching darkness. "It feels like a club that no one wants to belong to."

Judy chuckled softly, her eyes tracing the invisible path of a distant firefly. "A club of the heartbroken, you mean?"

"Exactly."

I retired to my room a little after nine, where I sat on the edge of my bed, my mind still turning over Judy's words like a rough stone smoothed by ripples in a brook. Outside, the moon beamed overhead, a silver orb casting a soft luminescence over the dunes that stretched out beyond the yard.

Staring out into the night, my thoughts drifted back to my past. The images came as fleeting ghosts, some more solid than others—soft smiles and laughter, shared secrets and quiet whispers—glimpses of the years now behind me. In the distance, the lighthouse's brilliant beam cut through the darkness, a silent sentinel protecting the shores. As a young woman, I'd sit for hours watching that beacon, captivated by its rhythmic pulse. Looking upon it now, that same sense of wonder washed over me.

As if in response to my memories, the lighthouse's light

seemed to dance and twirl, painting the darkness with streaks of silver and white. The past and the present felt like they were converging in this singular moment, a siren's song pulling me from my daydream.

CHAPTER 4

Monday

The next morning came early. As I blinked open my eyes, I was greeted by the sun slowly peeking over the watery horizon. The vivid painting of orange and pink in the eastern sky was a stark contrast to the deep blues and silvers of the previous night. I rose slowly, the weight of yesterday's conversations still heavy on my shoulders. It had been a long time since I had talked about my life in Sims Chapel, about Mother, and about Jack. But I needed to get this off my chest, to liberate myself from the shackles that had bound me for so long.

The house was silent as I made my way down the hall. Seeing that I was the first one up, I retreated to the library, where I picked up my copy of The Great Gatsby and lost myself for a while within its pages. The characters' lives seemed so distant from my own, yet there was something in their longing, their struggle for identity and acceptance, that rang true.

As I immersed myself in the world of Jay Gatsby and Nick Carraway, the house began to stir. Judy wandered in first, her hair in disarray. She sank into the armchair across from me, cradling her head in her hands.

"It's too early," she mumbled, rubbing her eyes.

I watched her with an amused smile, setting my book face down on the coffee table.

Diane arrived then through the back door, the sound of her footsteps echoing down the hall. I paused for a moment, listening as her heels clacked against the hardwood.

I left Judy in the library and found Diane in the kitchen, her dark hair tied back in a neat bun, grabbing a bagel from the breadbox. She didn't notice me at first, and I let her be. I put on a pot of tea, the gentle hissing of the kettle a comforting background noise. When it came to a boil, I poured it over the waiting teabag and fixed a cup for Diane too.

"Morning," I said as I approached her, the steaming mugs in hand.

"Oh, morning," she said, taking the mug from me. "Thank you." She sipped the tea slowly.

"You seem distracted this morning. Is everything all right?"

"Mmm? Sorry, just thinking."

"Anything in particular?" I asked, not pushing but showing my willingness to listen.

She remained silent for a few seconds, her gaze far away. Then she looked at me, her eyes clear and strong. "It's Cassie. She's having trouble at school. Fighting with her classmates, getting into arguments with her teachers. She's having difficulty adjusting to the fact that Kyle is gone. I've tried to talk to her, to help her understand, but..."

I placed my tea on the counter and moved closer to her, laying a steadying hand on her shoulder. Her face softened at the contact, and she turned to me, her eyes so full of worry that it pained me.

"Do you want to talk about it? Despite what you might have heard about me being cold and distant, I'm actually a good listener."

My words drew a smile from Diane, and she gave a quiet chuckle, her tension unfurling slightly. "It's nothing to burden you with, really. I guess she just needs more time, you know?"

I did know. "Most people say that time heals all wounds, but they often forget to mention how unpredictable that time can be. Or the fact that sometimes, the wound closes up but leaves a scar that never really fades."

"I just don't know what else to do for her. Losing Kyle has been the most difficult thing I've ever had to go through. But it's not just about me. Watching Cassie hurting, it's...heartbreaking. You see, I was a teenager when I had her, so I know what it's like to struggle. Now, seeing her have her own issues, it feels like I've come full circle."

I nodded, understanding her feelings completely. "It's tough, especially when you feel like you're not able to help the person you love the most. But remember, Diane, grief isn't linear. We all heal at different rates and in different ways. Give her some more time. I'm sure she'll start to turn the corner soon enough. And if not, there's always professional help."

After breakfast, we returned to the library to pick up where we'd left off the previous evening. Now that Diane had composed herself, she settled into the armchair and turned on the tape recorder.

"Where were we? Oh yes, I remember." She put a finger in the air. "We were discussing your childhood. I have a pretty good feel for those early days, but I want to know about your teenage years. Were they as tumultuous as most?"

I gave a laugh as I drifted back to that time. "Tumultuous? That's one way to put it."

Sims Chapel, TN

May 1949

My mother's voice echoed through the dense woods, calling me home for supper.

"Sorry," I said as I got to my feet and brushed the dirt from my faded blue jeans. "I gotta go. If I'm late again, Mother will tan my hide."

Jack reeled in his line and carefully secured the hook. "That's okay. I promised my mama I'd be home before dark too."

We gathered our gear—fishing rods, tackle, and bait—and hiked out of the woods together. When we reached the top of the hill, I turned for home and said, "I guess I'll see you tomorrow."

"As long as the good Lord's willing. Don't forget, George gave me tomorrow off, so I plan on casting a line bright and early."

"I haven't forgotten," I said, offering him my best smile. "But thanks for reminding me."

As I walked through the front door of my house, Mother was waiting, hands on her hips. "Sara Anne Coffee, what have I told you about coming home late?"

"But I'm not late, Mama. I came as soon as you hollered. Besides," I said as I placed the fishing gear by the door, "I wasn't getting into any trouble. Jack and I were just fishing down at the creek."

"Again? How many days in a row does this make? Four? Five?"

Actually, it was six, but I decided it was best not to correct her.

"Something like that," I replied, my eyes downcast under her scrutiny. "But I got all my chores done, and I helped Mr. Sullivan clean out that old barn this afternoon, just like I said I would." I received a sigh in return, Mother's stern façade softening.

"Fine. As long as your chores were all done." She returned to cooking, pushing the bacon to one side of the pan while she cracked a few eggs into the hot grease. "But don't let me catch you shirking your duties. You hear? Not just so you can go hanging around with that Bennett boy all day. I'm still not crazy about you and him in the woods all alone for hours on end anyway. It ain't like it was when you were kids. You're eighteen now, and there's some things a young lady ought to be mindful of."

"Mother, Jack is just a friend. And I'm not some silly girl who's going to get herself into trouble. Besides that, Jack Bennett is the nicest boy in all of Sims Chapel. Probably the whole county. Everyone says so. Even Clara, and you know how good a judge of character she is."

"Well..." Her expression softened further, her stern gaze settling into something more benevolent. "Why don't we continue this conversation another time? Right now, you need to get in that bathroom and get washed up. I'll have supper on the table directly."

"Yes ma'am."

As I retreated to the bathroom, I wondered what my mother saw in Jack that the rest of the town seemed blind to. She had expressed her doubts about him before, but as I scrubbed my hands under the warm water, washing away the dirt and grime, I couldn't let go of my own strong feelings. As far as I was concerned, Jack Bennett hung the moon.

* * *

The next morning, I was up and at it bright and early, sweeping floors, dusting shelves, and scrubbing surfaces until they gleamed in the sunlight. I moved with determination, my slender frame stretching and bending, tirelessly working until my inside chores were done.

Afterward, I strolled around the backyard garden dotted with marigolds and tulips. I touched the flowers gently as if they were made of glass, whispering words of encouragement to the budding beauties. The flowers seemed to respond to my touch, swaying along to the sound of my voice. My eyes widened in delight when I spotted a new sprout, pushing its way through the fertile soil. Kneeling down next to it, I brushed away some of the surrounding dirt, giving it more room to grow. "There you go, little one. Breathe, stretch, and reach for the sky."

I went back inside, wiping my dirt-streaked hands on my apron. With Mother at work, I longed for the woods, for the serene whispers of the wind through the trees and the comforting crunch of leaves underfoot. I loved the way the forest's dappled sunlight filtered through the towering pines, casting intricate patterns like lacework on the forest floor below. But more than that, I longed for time with Jack.

Ever since we first met when we were kids, there was an inexplicable bond between us, a friendship that had deepened over time. Jack, with his ruffled sandy-brown hair and ocean-blue eyes, had an allure that was hard to resist. He was a gentle soul, full of kindness and compassion, and he was the only person I knew who shared my love for the woods. And today, I felt that pull stronger than ever.

With my chores complete, I used the leftover bacon and

biscuits from the night before and prepared breakfast for me and Jack. It was half past eight, which meant he would be at the creek by now. As I packed the food, my heart fluttered in anticipation, and a soft smile lingered on my lips.

"I thought I might find you here," I called as I spotted Jack crouched near the edge of the creek.

He looked up at the sound of my voice and smiled. "You're early. No chores today?"

"Already finished them," I replied, then sat down beside him on the rock. "I brought us something to eat, if you're hungry. It isn't much—just some bacon and biscuits."

"Thanks. I can always count on you."

We spent the next few minutes talking about everything and nothing in particular, just enjoying each other's company.

"Did you make it home in time last night?" Jack asked as he finished the last of his biscuit.

"Barely. But Mama still almost had a fit."

"She's not still giving you trouble about us fishing together, is she?"

"You know how she is, Jack. She just worries."

He faced me, his eyes full of understanding. "I get it. My mama's the same way. Always fretting over something or another."

We sat for a while, listening to the sounds of nature around us—the chirping birds overhead, the rustling leaves under the soft breeze, and the steady flow of water against the rocks.

"I've been thinking," Jack said. "Remember how you told me you'd be willing to help me and George around the dock? I mentioned it to him, and he thinks it's a fine idea."

"Really?"

"We're thinking of adding a new section to make it suitable

for more boats, and we could sure use an extra pair of hands, even if they're as delicate as yours," he said, poking me playfully in the side.

I swatted his hand away but couldn't hide my smile. "Yeah, that'd be great. Oh," I said, thinking of my chores. "I'd still have to get my work done at home. Maybe I could do that first thing, then come to the dock after. What time would you need me there?"

"Noon. George and I start early, but we take a break around then. It'd give you more than enough time to finish your chores."

"That sounds fine. I'll still need to get Mama's okay, but it shouldn't be a problem. Tell George I'll do it."

"You're a lifesaver, Sara." Jack's whole demeanor seemed to lighten after that, the promise of additional assistance on the dock clearly serving to alleviate some of his stress.

I laughed, brushing off the compliment with the back of my hand. "I'm no such thing. Besides, I'm glad to help, and it'll give me something to do in the afternoons. Sitting up there in that house all day can be maddening."

"I know what you mean," he said as he checked his line. "If I wasn't working for George, I'd go stir-crazy."

As the afternoon wore on, we pulled dozens of fish from the creek, our laughter ringing through the woods as each fish squirmed and flipped on the end of the poles. My hands became a mess of scales and mud, but I didn't mind. I was too immersed in the simple joy of the moment, and the thrill of the new adventure waiting for me on the dock. Now, all I had to do was sell the idea to Mother.

CHAPTER 5

It took three days and a lot of begging, but Mother finally relented.

"All right, Sara Anne," she said one evening as she brushed a loose curl from my face. "If you promise not to let this dock business interfere with your chores, then you can help Jack and George."

I squealed in delight, throwing my arms around her in a grateful hug. "Oh, thank you! You don't know how much this means to me."

"I only hope you know what you're getting yourself into."

"I do, Mother. I'm up for it, really. I'm a hard worker, and I don't mind getting my hands dirty."

She pulled back and looked at me. "That's not what I meant, sweet girl."

I looked into her worried eyes, not fully understanding the depth of her concern. I knew she had reservations about me spending so much time with Jack, but I was too excited to worry about that. "Mama, Jack's a good guy. He wouldn't do anything to hurt me."

"I know you believe that, but hearts can be fragile. Especially at your age. Just be careful, that's all I'm saying."

My mother had been through her fair share of heartbreaks, and she knew what they could do to a person, changing them from hopeful and bright, to guarded and wary. Still, I didn't see any reason to worry. Life was exciting, and I wanted to live every minute of it.

The following week, I started work on the dock. Jack and George taught me the ropes, everything from fixing loose boards to cleaning boats. The work was grueling, the summer sun turning my skin the color of molasses, but I loved every minute of it. And the best part was the company. Jack and George were an odd pair to say the least. George, with his gruff exterior but heart as big as the lake, and Jack with his quick wit and infectious laughter. They made me feel like I belonged in a world where girls my age didn't typically venture.

Most times, I'd sit and listen as they went back and forth with their banter. But sometimes I'd join in, earning my fair share of laughter. The dock became my second home, a place where I could be myself.

But every now and then, when I'd catch myself staring at Jack, my mother's words would echo in the back of my mind. Jack was so effortlessly charming that people were drawn to him, and I was no exception. There were moments when his eyes would meet mine, lingering for just a breath longer than they should have. Moments when his hands brushed against mine as we worked side by side, sending a jolt of electricity through me. His smile was genuine and contagious, stirring emotions inside me that I had never felt before.

Time seemed to move differently whenever Jack was around. Days felt too short, nights too long. His laughter echoed in my dreams, his lake-soaked scent lingering on my clothes long after our work was done. I found myself daydreaming about him during quiet moments, his face as vivid in my mind as the sun setting over the lake.

Despite my mother's warning, my feelings for Jack were

growing stronger, like a wildflower blooming in an open field. They were wild and uncontrollable, deepening in color with each passing day. I knew I was on the brink of something indescribable, something that could be beautiful or devastating, or maybe even both at the same time.

Some nights, I'd sit at the edge of the dock, my bare feet dangling over the side into the cool water as the horizon swallowed the sun. Those were the moments when I would let my thoughts wander, tracing Jack's features in my mind, reliving our conversations. Jack would often join me, sitting quietly at my side. His closeness was comforting, his presence alone able to quiet my mind.

When we did speak, our conversations flowed naturally as they always did, effortless and familiar. We'd chat about the day's work, the latest town gossip, and our hopes and dreams. There was never talk of love, no passionate declarations or star-crossed promises. Our connection was not rooted in grand gestures but was instead built on quiet companionship and a mutual understanding that ran deeper than words could reach. This unspoken bond between us was far more compelling than any romantic novel. It was in the way he looked at me, and in the way he touched my shoulder when he passed me, a simple gesture that sent delicate shivers down my spine.

I was acutely aware of his presence, drawn to him like a ship to a lighthouse in the darkness. He was a silent beacon in the night, a magnet that tugged at the strings of my heart with an irresistible force.

We had become a part of each other's lives, a constant anchor in the ebb and flow of everyday existence. I could no more imagine a day without him than I could envision a night without stars. The tranquility of our shared moments felt hauntingly fragile, like the thin frost on an early winter morning, beautiful yet so easily shattered with a simple touch. The fear of losing what we had clung to my heart in the lonely hours of the night. I would lie awake, staring at the vast expanse of the starlit sky, hoping and praying that our moment would last forever.

Present

"Did Jack ever reciprocate your feelings?"

Diane's voice brought me back to the present, her question piercing through my reminiscence. I was momentarily lost, unsure of how to verbalize the complex web of emotions that had intertwined Jack and me.

"Not in words, but...in actions, in looks. In the way he'd listen to me, truly listen, when nobody else would."

"Did you consider Jack your boyfriend?"

"No," I replied with a shake of my head. "Not in those early days. We were never so conventional. We were ... companions. Friends. Allies in a world that often felt too large and too small all at once."

Diane studied me in that probing way of hers, her eyebrows knitted together in a thoughtful arch. She took a slow sip of her coffee, her gaze unyielding.

"Do you regret not telling him how you felt?"

Regret. That word had cast long shadows over my heart. I had reasons for the choices I made, for the words I left unsaid. Yet, they seemed infinitesimally small in the face of what might have been.

"I don't know," I admitted. "Sometimes, I think if I had

told him outright, if I'd been honest with him, we could have had more. Or we could have lost everything."

Sims Chapel, TN

July 1949

I drew a hand across my forehead, wiping the sweat from my brow. "School starts in just a few weeks. Are you looking forward to it?"

"You know I've never been one for school," said Jack as he checked his line.

"Well, I'm looking forward to it. I've been thinking about what I want to focus on while I'm in college, and I think I've decided on math."

Jack adjusted his ball cap. "Math? But I thought you wanted to be a lawyer?"

"I did, once," I replied, digging my toes into the cool dirt. "But I realized that numbers...mathematics, it feels like home. Plus, I don't have to stand up in front of people and talk, which is a bonus. You know how nervous I get."

"Yeah, I remember the school spelling bee in eighth grade. You were shaking like a leaf."

I groaned at the memory. "Don't remind me."

"So math, huh?" he mused. "Yeah, that's suits you well. You're certainly smart enough, and you've always had a knack for numbers. Maybe you can put it to good use someday—be a teacher or something."

"Maybe. So, what are you going to do when school is over? Do you ever think about going to college?"

Jack laughed. "I can barely stomach high school. No sir, once I graduate next spring, I'm going to work. I've got my sights set on a place like Clara's one day. Which means I'll need to start making some money right away."

"Does that mean you won't be around next summer?" The thought of him leaving filled me with a sudden dread.

He didn't reply immediately, keeping his gaze on the dancing reflections of sunlight scattered by the water. "Naw, I reckon I'll still be here, at least for one more summer. I already promised George I'd be around to help him. And a man should always keep his promises."

"Right," I said, the knot in my chest loosening. I took in my surroundings—the murky water, the emerald green mountains, the sound of the wind rustling through the tall cottonwood trees. "You know, I'm really going to miss this."

"What?"

"This." I gestured to the water, the trees. "Fishing, working on the dock with you and George ... spending time with you. Far and away, this has been the best summer of my life."

A smile worked its way onto Jack's face. "Yeah, it has been pretty great, hasn't it?"

"Since you're planning on helping George next summer, do you think I could help too?"

Jack shrugged a shoulder. "I don't see why not. George ain't going nowhere, and neither is the work."

"Good. I'm already looking forward to it."

He looked at me then, his eyes filled with warmth. "You know, it won't be the same without you here. For as long as I can remember, it's always been me and you against the world. Now, you're going off to college. Don't know how I'll manage without you."

I blinked in surprise, not expecting his words.

"Ever since Lewis died, you're the closest friend I've got," he added, his fingers fidgeting with the lures in his tackle box.

Overwhelmed by his confession, I grasped for words. "Jack... I—"

"It's okay," he interrupted, a faint blush creeping onto his cheeks. "You ain't got to say anything."

But I couldn't let his sentiment go unacknowledged. After all, I had been waiting a long time to hear him say something like that. "No, Jack, I want to. I know how much your brother meant to you. So to hear you say that I'm your closest friend, well...that means a lot. And just so you know, you're my closest friend too, and..."

The moment was broken when a fish tugged at Jack's line. He reached out and steadied the rod, his eyes once again filled with that familiar spark. I had seen that expression countless times over the summer, one that I was convinced I would never forget.

"Will you look at that? A nice red-eye," he said, grinning with pride as he got the fish to the bank. He unhooked it carefully, holding it up against the midday sun. "This one will make a fine supper."

I watched Jack working on another catch and found myself smiling. I was grateful for these moments by his side—the feel of the earth beneath us, the sound of the rushing water, and Jack's laughter filling up each gap in between.

When the sun began to set and we prepared to leave, I turned toward him. "Jack..."

"Hmm?"

My heart fluttered. I had been thinking about this moment for weeks, ever since Mama's comments about Jack and I spending too much time together. I took a deep breath and said, "You know how Mother worries about us being together?"

Jack nodded slowly, looking serious. "Yeah, I know."

"Sometimes I wonder," I trailed off again before finally gathering the courage. "Do you ever think about...us?"

"Us? What do you mean?"

"You know, beyond fishing and working together?" My voice was barely above a whisper, my heart pounding in my chest as I waited for his response.

Jack stopped packing up his gear and turned toward me. He broke into one of his warm smiles and simply said, "Every day, Sara Coffee. Every single day."

That night, as I lay in bed staring out the window at the world bathed in silver, a new sense of hope and anticipation bloomed within me. Staring at the moon, I whispered to myself, "Every day," and fell asleep with a smile on my face.

CHAPTER 6

Present

Diane gave me a look of gentle sadness, her brow slightly wrinkled with thoughtful consideration. "It sounds like you really loved him."

"Yes, I did," I said, recalling how deeply I had fallen for Jack that summer. "More than anything." Remembering Jack—his laughter, the way his blue eyes shimmered in the sunlight— felt like poking at an old wound. It hurt, but there was a comforting familiarity in the pain.

"Speaking of Jack...wasn't he the reason you landed in Kitty Hawk in the first place? In my research for this week, I came across a transcript of an interview you did years ago with the Charlotte observer, where you mentioned him as being the reason you left home."

I nodded once, my thoughts drifting. "But it wasn't just him. There were many factors that led to my leaving."

Diane leaned back in her chair, inspecting my face as if searching for a hint of some hidden truth. "Like what?"

"For starters, there was the sheer monotony of life back home. Every day was the same people, the same conversations, the same landscapes. Not to mention I was struggling with my career choice. I enjoyed being a teacher, at first, but as time went on I found it wasn't what I'd dreamed of. The kids were great, but the bureaucracy was suffocating, and there was no room for creativity, no space for spontaneity. It was disheartening to say the least."

"I see." Diane jotted down notes in her notepad, her brows drawn together for a second before she finally looked up at me again. "So, whatever happened between you and Jack? Did you ever work up the nerve to tell him how you felt or did the secret wither away with time?"

I shifted my gaze to an old black-and-white photo on the wall. The only tangible memory of me and Jack, arm in arm when we were teenagers. It had been taken a few days before I left for college. "Yes," I admitted, a lump forming in my throat. "I told him. But it took a few words of encouragement and an unforgettable sunset to coax it out of me."

Sims Chapel, TN

August 1949

"Sara, what brings you by?" George asked one evening as he was closing up shop.

"I was hoping to talk to you, if you have a minute."

"For you, course I do." He offered me a seat in the shack and a glass of sweet tea. "What's on your mind, darlin'?"

I took a deep breath, tracing the rim of my tea glass. "George, I've been thinking...about Jack."

"What about Jack? He's not in some kind of trouble, is he?"

I shook my head, my lips pressing together in a tight line as I searched for the right words. "No...it's just...I kinda like him, you see, and I don't exactly know how to tell him. And since you know him better than just about anyone, I thought you might have an idea."

George leaned back in his chair, his face relaxing. "Oh. And here I was worrying it was something serious."

"This is serious, George," I protested. "At least to me. I've been trying all summer to work up the courage to tell him, but no matter how hard I try, the words just won't come."

"I'm sorry." George's grin softened into a warm smile. "I didn't mean to belittle your feelings. When it comes to Jack, he...well, he's not the easiest to read. But I can tell you this—he thinks mighty highly of you."

"He does?"

"Of course. You should see how his face lights up whenever someone mentions your name. I'm no mind reader, but if that ain't a sign of affection, I don't know what is."

A blush crept across my cheeks.

"But if you really wanna know how he feels, talk to him, and be truthful. Jack, he values honesty above all else. You, of all people, should know that."

I was silent as I absorbed his words, my mind swirling with thoughts of Jack. I finally nodded, meeting George's gaze. "Honesty," I said, my fingers absently tracing the condensation on my tea glass. "I'm sure you're right. It's just... What if he doesn't feel the same way?"

George shrugged. "Then he doesn't. And that will sting, no doubt about it. But at least you'll know where you stand. Who knows? Maybe he feels the same way, and you're worried for nothing. Sometimes, the fear of rejection outweighs the possibility of happiness. But what's most important is that you stay true to yourself and your feelings. If he can't reciprocate, it's not because you're at fault, but because his feelings are different.

And that's okay."

I listened to George, his words resonating deep within me. Something shifted, a slow unearthing of a courage I didn't realize I had. "You're right," I said, the words leaving me in a rush. "I have to tell him."

George smiled at me, the kind of smile that made you feel like you've accomplished something great. "That's the spirit," he said, lifting his glass in a silent toast to my newfound resolution.

* * *

Later that night, I lay in bed, replaying George's words in my head. Jack. Honesty. Rejection. Happiness. The fear of rejection was something I had always battled with, a lurking shadow that kept me silent about my deepest feelings. But now, the possibility of happiness seemed worth the risk. Jack was a young man who made me laugh, who listened when I spoke and saw me for who I truly was. I thought of his warm smile, his endless eyes that seemed to hold a world of mystery I yearned to unravel. Yes, I decided, he was worth the risk.

The following day dawned bright and beautiful, with an intensity that mirrored my own resolve. Buoyed by George's supportive words, I found myself striding toward the lake with a fierceness I didn't know I possessed. I had dressed in my favorite blouse, a soft pastel pink that complemented my complexion and had me brimming with confidence. The closer I got to the water, the faster my heart raced, but I did not let the fear deter me.

At the edge of the lake, where the creek merged with the water, I found Jack hunched over his journal, deep in thought.

"Whatcha working on?"

He looked up as I approached. "Oh, nothing. Just doing a

little writing," he said, closing the journal and tucking it away.

"Are you working on another story?"

Jack shook his head. "Actually, I was thinking about Lewis."

"Oh." I sat down beside him on the grassy bank. "Do you want to talk about it?"

"No, not really. I just... I miss him, you know?"

I nodded, not quite knowing what to say. "I can only imagine," I said, placing my hand over his.

He glanced at our intertwined hands, then back at me, his eyes reflecting the same vulnerability he always hid behind his mischievous grin. He sighed, a deep weary sound that seemed to echo across the lake. "Sometimes, I feel like I'm the only one who remembers him. Like if I stop, he'll just...fade away."

"I don't think memories work like that, Jack. Mother says that memories are resilient, like people. They aren't tied to the number of people who remember, but to the strength of the emotions they evoke. I think Lewis will always be a part of you, no matter what. He'll always be a part of me too."

Jack was silent for a moment, studying the rippling water as if it held the answers to the questions he was too afraid to ask. "I guess you're right," he finally said, his gaze shifting back to me. "I just worry that I'm not doing him justice. That by not talking about him, I'm failing him in some way."

I shifted closer, the grass whispering softly around us. "Grief is a strange thing. There's no right or wrong way to handle it. You're not failing Lewis by not talking about him all the time."

His lips tightened, a faint line appearing between his brows. Just then, a gentle breeze rustled through the trees, carrying with it the scent of evening blooms. We sat there, shoulder to shoulder, as the sun began to dip beneath the horizon.

"I think that Lewis would have liked this moment," Jack said. "The tranquility of the lake, the colors of the sunset. He always found peace in nature."

I observed him, his profile etched against the dying light of the day. "He'd be glad to know you're finding peace here too. Lewis would want you to remember him, of course, but also to live your life. To find joy wherever you can."

There was another long pause, broken a moment later when Jack turned to me and said, "So, what are you all gussied up for this evening?"

I'd nearly forgotten what I was wearing. I glanced down at the sleeveless blouse I had chosen, the one with the delicate lace border that Jack had always admired. "Oh, this?" I smoothed my hands over the material self-consciously. "I just wanted to feel like a girl today."

Jack raised an eyebrow, his gaze lingering on me longer than usual. "You certainly look like one. You always do clean up nice."

His words stirred something in me, a strange mix of pleasure and surprise. Jack wasn't usually one for compliments. I let out a soft chuckle, shaking my head slightly. "You think so?"

"Sure."

My cheeks flushed, a warmth spreading through me. Despite the cool evening air, I felt a sudden heat that had nothing to do with the remnants of the day's sunlight. "Thank you, Jack. That's nice of you to say."

His eyes met mine, the corners of his mouth lifting slightly in a half-smile. "You're welcome."

For a few long seconds, we just looked at each other. His gaze was soft yet held a certain intensity that stirred my heart.

I felt compelled to say something, anything, but I sat there, my words caught in my throat. In the ensuing quiet, the sounds of nature grew louder—the wind through the trees, the distant call of a bird.

When the moment had passed, Jack turned his attention back to the lake. "It's a beautiful evening, isn't it?"

I followed his gaze out toward the water, the setting sun casting rays of gold and orange that danced across its surface. "Yes, it certainly is."

"I reckon I could spend the rest of my life right here on this bank, looking at sunsets like this. I know some folks want fortune and fame, but not me. Simple pleasures like the chirping of crickets and good company are all I need."

I was speechless again. His sentiment was so sincere, so genuine that it caught me off guard. "Jack," I began, hesitating before going on. "Can I ask you something?"

"Sure."

I swallowed, my heart pounding against my chest as if it was trying to find its way out. The question I'd held back for so long threatened to choke me, but I managed to push it out in a breathless whisper. "Would you ever want me to be a part of those simple pleasures?"

"Of course I would," he answered without hesitation. "I reckon you and I will always be friends."

His words were comforting, yet they sent a pang of disappointment through my heart. Friends. Just friends. I nodded slowly, forcing a smile onto my face. I wanted to ask another question, to dig deeper, to make him understand I was talking about more than mere friendship, but I didn't. I couldn't. The fear of rejection was too much for my heart to take. Instead, I watched the sun set deeper into the lake, each second passing like an eternity. I longed for him to understand the truth behind my words, to understand the depth of my feelings. But, as the last rays of light faded and twilight began to creep in, I realized that it wasn't time for such revelations.

At dusk, we hiked through the woods until we reached the fork in the road. And just like always, Jack went one way and I the other. But before we parted, I turned to him and said, "I was hoping we could go out on the water one last time before I leave for school. You know, for old times' sake."

Jack paused, a shadow of uncertainty dimming his eyes. He glanced at me, then back to the path leading to his house. He seemed to consider the possibilities for a moment. "Sure," he finally said. "How about tomorrow evening, after work? We can bring the fishing gear if you want, maybe try our luck at snagging one last catfish."

"Tomorrow is fine, but let's leave the gear. I've already caught my fair share of fish this summer. I just want to ride around and take in the scenery one last time, if that's all right."

His nod was slow, thoughtful. "All right, just the scenery it is."

As he walked away, his figure growing smaller in the fading light, a pang of sorrow clenched my heart. Tomorrow would be bittersweet, a final farewell to the lake that held so many precious memories.

That night, I stayed up later than normal, watching the moon rise high into the star-studded sky. I'd done it again—chickened out, too afraid to voice my true feelings. It was the same old tug of war between my heart and my fear. But as I lay there, I made a promise to myself. Tomorrow, I would tell Jack everything. No more hiding, no more pretending. Just the raw, unfiltered truth.

CHAPTER 7

The next day seemed to drag on as I went about my chores. My mind wandered constantly, to Jack, to the lake, to the words that I had yet to voice.

Yvonne called just after noon, and we talked for a good while. Her voice was a comforting distraction, yet even she seemed to sense my preoccupation.

"You're awfully quiet today," she said.

"Just thinking," I replied, my voice far away. But Yvonne wasn't easily fooled, knowing me as she did.

"Are you thinking about Jack again?"

"Maybe," I admitted, not realizing until that moment how tightly I was clutching the phone.

"Like I've told you a thousand times this summer, just go for it."

"You say that as if it's the simplest thing in the world."

She chuckled. "Because it is. You're just making it harder than it needs to be. Besides, you two were made for each other. Anyone can see that."

I exhaled, staring blankly at the dishes I was supposed to be rinsing. She was right, of course. Yvonne always had a way of cutting straight through the fog that clouded my thoughts.

"You really think so?"

"I know so," she replied. "Listen, I gotta go. But think about what I said, okay? And if you do decide to tell him how you feel, give me a call later. I want to know everything."

I nodded, even though she couldn't see me, my pulse quickening. "I will. Thanks, Yvonne." As we hung up, her words—just go for it—echoed in my mind.

Later that afternoon, as the sun began to dip, I set out for the dock. When I arrived, Jack had a cooler in one hand and a blanket in the other. Seeing him was like a release valve for the pressure that had been building up within me all day.

"Hey," he said, slipping the blanket under his arm and regarding me with a wave. "Are you ready for this?"

I hesitated for a moment, the words I had rehearsed all day suddenly slipping away. "I am."

He seemed to sense my apprehension, his gaze softening as he reached out to gently take my hand. "Everything okay?"

I squeezed his hand in silent reassurance, offering a weak smile.

We boarded the boat then and set off on our final voyage as friends. One way or another, the day would end with a changed relationship between us. I looked out onto the rippling waters and inhaled deeply. The lake had always been our refuge, our sanctuary. And now, it would bear witness to this pivotal moment in our relationship.

As the boat glided smoothly over the glassy surface, Jack broke the silence. "You remember the first time we came here?" His voice was a soft whisper against the gentle hum of the boat's engine as we passed the sand bar.

I nodded, unable to trust myself to speak. I remembered it all too well—our laughter as we splashed in the water, the thrill of our shared adventure. Those memories seemed like echoes from another lifetime now, their sweetness tinged with a bitter aftertaste. As we continued up the lake, my mind wandered back to all the times we had spent here, to all the secrets we had shared, the dreams we had fostered. The lake held our past. It was a part of us, and now it was set to become a part of our future, whatever that may be.

Part of me wanted to believe that Jack felt the same about me as I did him, that my imagination wasn't just playing tricks on me. After all, there had been signs—the gentle brush of his hand against mine, stolen glances when he thought I wasn't looking, his habit of lingering just a bit too long in my company. It was the kind of evidence that was easy to dismiss, easy to explain away as nothing more than the polite attentions of a good friend. But there was something about the way he looked at me, something disarming in his gaze that made my heart flutter and my mind race with possibilities. But the other part of me worried that I was reading too much into it, that my heart was seeing what it wanted to see, and that I was on the brink of making a terrible mistake, one that would shatter our friendship forever.

Jack cut back on the engine, breaking my thoughts. When we reached the bridge, he cut off the engine and anchored. All around us, the world stilled.

"What is this place?"

"George told me about this spot once... Said it was the perfect place to see the sun set. I thought you might appreciate it."

I tried to hide the surprise on my face. Jack had remembered my random musings about sunsets and their calming, mesmerizing beauty. I blinked back tears that welled up suddenly. My heart was full of feelings, uncertain and hopeful at the same time. "Yes, it does look like the perfect spot, doesn't it? You know, I remember the first time you took me fishing. It was back there, wasn't it?" I pointed to a spot farther down the lake, where the willow hung low.

Jack glanced over his shoulder before looking at me. "Yeah. You were scared of worms, remember?"

"Yes, I remember." I dropped my eyes, hiding my embarrassment. "Funny how things change. Speaking of change, there's something I've been meaning to tell you."

"Yes?" he asked, his attention momentarily torn away from the horizon.

"I ...well...I've been thinking...about us...about how we've changed. It feels like only yesterday that we were kids, running around in the woods, fishing in the creek. Now look at us, both all grown up. Where has the time gone?"

Jack let out a soft chuckle. "Time has a way of slipping by, doesn't it? And you're right, we're all but grown-ups now."

A sudden surge of anxiety washed over me. My instinct was to end the conversation there or change the subject, but I had put this off long enough. It was now or never.

"And that's just it, Jack... We've known each other for so long, been through so much together. I think it's time for me to be honest, not just with you, but with myself too." I took a deep breath, finding it impossible to say the words that had been on my mind for months. I tried to come up with an excuse, a half-hearted lie, but instead I leaned forward and closed the distance between us. As our lips met, all my doubts disappeared in an instant. This felt right, I thought, as the kiss deepened. My body was on fire, and I never wanted this moment to end.

When we finally pulled away, I searched Jack's eyes for any sign that he felt the same way about the kiss as I did. For a brief moment, I thought I saw a flicker—of excitement, relief, or hope. But it quickly vanished.

"What was that?" he asked, his face twisted with shock and bewilderment.

"I'm... I'm sorry," I said, fumbling for words. "You didn't like it?"

Jack quickly looked away before bringing his eyes back to me. "It's not that I didn't like it, Sara. It's just... Why did you do it?"

Oh God, what have I done? My mind raced with guilt and regret at his question. "I...I don't know," I stammered, my heart beating so fast I thought it might burst. "I just... I thought that..."

"You thought what?"

"I thought that maybe...you liked me. You know, more than as a friend."

Jack leaned back in his seat and ran a hand through this hair. I watched him silently, my stomach twisting with anxiety.

"Sara..." He looked at me, his eyes shimmering in the dusky light. "Sara, of course I like you."

"You do?"

"But..." He broke eye contact. "But it's...complicated."

His statement made my hopeful heart sink again. It was a familiar phrase—"it's complicated." It was an excuse used by people who were unwilling or unable to commit.

"Why is it complicated, Jack?"

He looked away into the distance, his silence unbearable. I wanted answers but feared I had opened a door that couldn't be closed again.

"Because...I like things the way they are. And I don't want to ruin our friendship." The weight of his words hung heavy in the air like a thick fog, making it hard for me to breathe.

"But, maybe we could have something more," I said softly, my voice filled with a desperate plea. I dared to reach out and touch his hand, which was resting on his knee. His fingers were cold compared to mine.

Jack looked back at me then, the color having drained from his face. For a moment he did not pull away from my touch, but then he gently slipped his hand out from under mine.

"Sara," he began, pausing as though searching for the right words, or perhaps the courage to say them. "I value what we have too much to risk it over something uncertain."

I wanted to protest, to tell him that life is all about taking risks, especially when it involves matters of the heart. But somehow I couldn't summon the strength to utter those words. Instead I gave him a weak smile through my unshed tears and simply nodded.

Jack's posture relaxed and the color slowly returned to his face. But even as he smiled back at me, sadness clouded his features. I thought I saw him open his mouth to speak again, but he quickly closed it and looked away, bringing an end to any chance I had of hearing him say the words I longed for.

CHAPTER 8

Present

"So Jack never reciprocated your feelings?" Diane asked, her eyes filled with the same sympathetic sadness I'd seen in so many faces over the years.

I shook my head with a weary smile. "Not in the way I wanted him to. He cared for me, deeply. Just not in the way I cared for him. We continued to be friends, and that was enough for him. But for me...it was never quite enough."

"And you never tried again?"

"Sure, I tried. But each time, it was like trying to hold water in my hands. It just slipped away." The memory of those attempts had left scars so deep that even now, it still had the power to hurt. "I moved on, eventually, but it took many years and a lot of heartache before I finally learned my lesson."

At half past five, we decided to call it quits. I was exhausted, and by the look of the dark circles under Diane's eyes, she was too. We'd had enough revelations and reminiscing for one day, and I longed for a hot meal and a good night's rest.

"Whatever became of Jack?" Diane asked as we tidied up and moved toward the kitchen. "Do you still keep in touch?"

I paused, my hands tightening around the dish I was holding. "No. We haven't spoken in a long time. Not since..." I faltered, not sure if I was ready to unpack the rest of the story.

"Not since what?"

"I guess you'll have to wait until tomorrow to find out, won't you?" I said, attempting a lightness that I didn't quite feel.

Diane seemed to sense my unease and offered a gentle nod. "All right. Tomorrow then."

* * *

Despite my exhaustion, sleep did not come easily that night. As I lay in bed, moonlight streamed through the window, forming eerie shadows that danced around the room. The silence was deafening, broken only by the distant crashing of waves on the shore or the whip of the wind. I turned restlessly, trying to find a comfortable position, but the thoughts racing through my mind wouldn't let me. The ghost of Jack seemed to haunt every corner of my consciousness.

As I stared at the ceiling, memories rushed in like a tidal wave. His laugh, his voice, the sparkle in his eyes when he was excited about something. He was a vivid phantom, always just out of reach.

Tuesday

When dawn finally came, it slid in gently, the first rays of sunlight softening the edges of my sorrow. The world outside was waking up, and I could hear the quiet rustle of leaves as the wind played with them. Birds started singing their morning tunes, and for a moment, their cheerful chatter made me forget about Jack.

But then I remembered the conversation that lay ahead. The second part of Jack's and my story. The part that hurt the most. Was I ready to tell this tale?

Slowly, I got out of bed and walked to the window. The sun had just begun its ascent over the horizon, producing a warm golden glow that overspread the world. I watched as life began to stir outside. A couple of early joggers passed by on the beach, their breaths creating small puffs in the cool morning air. A lone seagull spiraled upwards, its cries echoing off the nearby dunes. Despite the heaviness in my heart, I was entranced by the beauty of the morning. The world continued to turn regardless of personal hardships and pain. Life went on.

Breakfast was a quiet affair. I poured myself a cup of coffee, the steam curling up into the air. I sipped it slowly, letting the bitter warmth spread through me, grounding me in a reality that seemed far too stark in the harsh light of day. The toast sat untouched on my plate, the butter slowly melting into it.

Diane appeared next, a mug of tea cradled in her hands. Her hair was pulled back into a messy bun, and she was wearing a round pair of reading glasses.

"Morning?" she asked as she entered. "Did you sleep well?"

I shook my head, the words lodging in my throat. She didn't need an answer. The bags under my eyes were probably telling enough.

"Do you want to push our conversation to the afternoon? There's plenty I could work on this morning."

"No. I want to do this. I need to do this." I took a sip of the hot coffee, letting the scalding liquid burn the roof of my mouth. "I hope you're finding the cottage cozy and comfortable."

"Yes, it's perfect, thank you. Between the plush mattress and the sound of the waves lulling me to sleep, I've slept better the past two nights than I have in months." She paused, her expression shifting from cheerful to somber in an instant. "As you can imagine, sleep has been elusive for me lately." A sadness crept into her eyes, and for a moment, I saw my own grief reflected back at me. There was a bond in our shared pain—a silent understanding of sleepless nights, the void that refused to be filled, and the heartache that came in waves.

"If you don't mind me asking, what happened...to your husband?"

Diane drew a ragged breath and exhaled slowly, her gaze dropping to her mug of tea. She traced the rim with a fingertip before she spoke. "It was a car accident. Stormy night, poor visibility... His death has been difficult to come to terms with, especially for Cassie. She's at that age where she needs her father the most."

"And how old is she?"

"Eleven...going on thirty."

I did the math in my head. "You don't look old enough to have a daughter that age."

"Thank you, but the sleepless nights and wrinkles beg to differ."

I was taken aback by her honesty, touched by her vulnerability. There was something about Diane that made me want to reach out and hug her, to tell her everything would be all right, though I knew it wouldn't. Instead, I settled for a reassuring smile.

* * *

After breakfast, we made our way out to the veranda that overlooked the sprawling green lawn and ocean. The sun was rising through the morning sky, its light glittering off the dew-dusted grass. Around us, a cool breeze blew, lightly kissing our faces.

Diane stood by the railing, looking out at the expanse of

the ocean. Her face was calm, her eyes distant. I watched her for a moment before moving to stand beside her.

"Beautiful, isn't it?"

She nodded without breaking her gaze. "It is. It's like the ocean never ends, just goes on and on forever."

"That's the beauty of it, isn't it? The endless possibilities. Just like life, it has its storms and its calm, its highs and its lows. But at the end of the day, it keeps going."

Diane's eyes glistened. "That's a beautiful way to put it. Is that what drew you to this place? The ocean, its endless possibilities?"

"Partly. Even when I was a child, I dreamed of seeing the ocean, of sitting on a sandy beach and listening to the waves crash against the shore. But it wasn't until I was about your age that I finally got up enough courage to make the journey."

Diane's forehead puckered. "But that would mean another twelve or thirteen years went by. What kept you?"

"Life, mostly. Responsibilities, fears, hope...you name it. But eventually, I realized that the only thing truly standing in my way was me."

* * *

"Years ago, you made a statement to the papers that said, and I quote, 'My entire life, everything that has happened to me, was predicated on that summer,'" Diane said when we had returned to the library. "Can you tell me more about that?"

I drew a breath, my gaze wandering away from Diane's prying eyes. No matter how much I hated to admit it—it always came back to that summer.

"To be honest, I thought that Jack and I would pick up where we left off, that things would be the same as they had before. Little did I know, that summer would change my life forever."

Sims Chapel, TN

May 1950

Glancing out the window of my dormitory, I contemplated the last nine months and how much I'd grown. Not just physically, but emotionally and mentally, too. My head was bursting with literature, philosophy, physics, and mathematics—the whole spectrum of an education that I had so longed for. For a small-town girl who had grown up tending gardens and mending clothes, this taste of knowledge was intoxicating.

Aside from my studies, I'd also made friends, genuine and close-knit friends who had taught me much about the world outside Sims Chapel. Like Mary, a physics major from Atlanta, who introduced me to the bustling life of the city through her stories. And Emily, an arts enthusiast from Chicago, who gave me my first taste of Impressionist paintings. They also happened to be my dorm mates, companions in this journey of exploration and self-discovery.

But no matter how hard I tried, thoughts of home crept into my mind, especially in the quiet moments when I was alone. I'd often think about the sound of my mother's voice, the woods around my house, and the water where once I had splashed and played without a care in the world. And inevitably, my thoughts would drift to Jack. What had he been up to all this time? Was he still at the water's edge, counting down the days until I returned? Or had he moved on and forgotten all about me?

I thought of his face—an intoxicating blend of boyish charm and rugged handsomeness that had captivated me from the beginning. His laughter danced in my memory, vibrant and warm, as if he were right there in the room with me. But before I allowed myself to fall under the spell of his memory, I shook my head, blinking away the vision. Jack might have been my past, but he wasn't my present, and he certainly wouldn't be my future. He'd made that crystal clear.

On the eve of summer break, I packed my suitcase with thoughts of home. Home, a place I longed for, a place where the scent of my mother's cooking filled the rooms with a comforting aroma, where I had spent endless summer afternoons running around the woods or navigating the lake with Jack. But after what happened the previous summer, would home ever feel the same again?

Two days later, I sat on my back porch, staring east toward the mountains. Once a peaceful backdrop to my childhood, the mountains now appeared as stoic sentinels, guarding secrets and memories that threatened to flood my mind. The air was rich with the scent of rain and pine, a heady mixture that reminded me of long hikes and lazy afternoons spent by the lake. I traced the grain of the wooden railing with my fingers, its familiar roughness grounding me in the present even as my thoughts strayed to the past. A soft breeze rustled through the trees, carrying the faint sound of water lapping against the shore. The lake was calling me, pulling me toward it with an invisible current.

"Is something on your mind?" Mother asked as she joined me on the porch.

"I'm just thinking." Her eyes searched my face for a moment

longer before she nodded, choosing not to press further.

"Have you given any thought to what you'll do this summer now that you're home?"

My instinct was to shrug off her question, to avoid the subject entirely, but the look in her eyes stopped me—a mix of worry and hope that made my heart twist uncomfortably. "I've been considering volunteering at the library or maybe finding a job in town."

"Does that mean you've decided against returning to the dock?"

The mention of the dock felt like a punch to the gut. I tried to keep my face blank, my eyes on the horizon, but I could feel them welling up with tears.

"I don't know," I said, swallowing hard. "I just don't know if I can go back there. Not after..." I hadn't told her about what happened last summer, about me kissing Jack and him rejecting me. Or about the guilt and regret that had been my constant companions since. But the long, penetrating stare she gave me told me she already knew, or at least suspected.

"Have you spoken to Jack since you got home?"

"No." The truth was I had been avoiding him. Our homes were less than a mile apart, separated by a stretch of dense forest, yet it felt like an ocean lay between us. There was no way to explain the aching emptiness that had settled in my heart. "I'm sure he's busy with his own life. The last thing he needs is me interrupting it."

She nodded, reaching over to pat my hand gently. Her touch was warm, offering comfort in the midst of my internal turmoil. "Sweetheart, I don't know what happened between you two, and frankly, it's none of my business, but if I might give you a piece of advice, don't let your heart become a harbor for regret. If you need to, talk things over with Jack. Mending friendships can be harder than mending hearts, but sometimes it's worth the struggle."

I considered that, letting her words seep into me like a warm cup of cocoa on a winter's day. "Thanks, Mama. I can always count on you to be the voice of reason."

She gave my hand a squeeze before standing up. "You're welcome, but remember, you're stronger than you think you are," she said, her words floating on the evening breeze like a lullaby. "And you're never alone."

With that, she disappeared into the house, leaving me with my thoughts.

CHAPTER 9

In the days that followed, I found myself wandering through the familiar woods around my house. The towering trees seemed to whisper secrets in the wind, their rustling leaves echoing memories of innocent laughter and carefree days. Every hidden hollow and mossy stone seemed to hold some remnant of our shared past. Jack and I had been inseparable once, two halves of a whole, each other's constant in a world that was ever-changing. Now, an invisible barrier divided us, as impenetrable as the densest forest.

* * *

One afternoon, while I sat on our old tree swing, Jack appeared. His figure emerged from between the trees like a ghost from the past, causing my heart to jump into my throat. His face was a mask of surprise, his eyes widening as he spotted me. For a moment, time seemed to stand still, the only sounds were the gentle creaking of the swing and the distant murmur of the stream.

"Hey," he said, his voice shattering the stillness.

"Hey."

"I was wondering when I might run into you. Connie told me you were back."

"Yeah," I replied, my eyes locked on his. "I got back a few

days ago. I've just been busy, that's all."

He took a step closer, his boots crunching on the carpet of fallen leaves. "So, how was school?"

"It was wonderful. I met so many great people and learned so many amazing things."

He let out a small laugh, a sound that I had missed more than I cared to admit. "That's good." He sat down beside me on the swing, his body just a whisper away from mine. The proximity was both familiar and foreign, bringing back a rush of memories that I had tried to bury deep within me. "Listen, I wanted to apologize...for the things I said when we last saw each other. I hurt you, and..."

I interrupted him, not ready for his apology, not yet. "It's okay, Jack. It was a long time ago." But as I spoke the words, I knew they weren't entirely true. The pain had dulled over time but was far from forgotten.

His eyes were a mix of regret and something else I couldn't quite decipher. "It's not okay, though. I should have handled things better. I just...was caught off guard, that's all. But I've had plenty of time to think about it since then, and I thought that maybe we could try again."

My heart gave a painful lurch. "What do you mean, try again?"

"I mean I'd like us to be friends again."

"Friends, huh?" Could we really go back to being friends after everything that had happened? Jack was not just a friend. He had been my first love, my first heartbreak, a chapter of my life that I had closed off and tucked away into a corner of my heart.

"Yeah. And who knows, maybe we can even be more than friends in the future."

More? Had I heard him correctly? My mind raced, trying to process his words. "Jack, I ... I don't know what to say."

"You don't have to say anything right now. Just think about it, okay?"

I studied him closely, noticing the slight lines around his eyes, the way the sun had weathered his skin. He was still the Jack I remembered, but also a man I barely knew.

"Okay, Jack. I will."

He squeezed my shoulder gently and stood up to leave. "Hey," he said, backing away. "It's good to have you back, Sara."

"Yeah." I took a deep breath, bracing myself for the emotional rollercoaster that I was about to embark on. "It's good to be back."

* * *

After that, we started to reconnect slowly, like two pieces of a fractured puzzle trying to find their match. We began by taking walks through the woods, or down to the lake, Jack telling me about the crowds of people he'd ferried to the islands, or the fish he'd caught the day before. I listened, nodding and laughing at his stories, while sharing some of my own. I told him about the books I had read, and the places I wanted to visit. The more time we spent together, the more I realized that even though we'd spent months apart, there was still a connection between us. A bond that was not easily severed.

As time went on, my old feelings for him resurfaced, but they were different now, matured in the way we had matured. Being in his presence was like coming home after a long journey—familiar, but new all the same.

There were moments, though, when the weight of our past descended upon us. When an innocent comment would stir up memories best forgotten, or a look would remind us of what I had done. We navigated those times with caution, like stepping over shards of glass scattered across a floor. But with each passing day, they became less frequent, more bearable. And for a while, things were like they had been, even better.

But all that changed one spring afternoon. It was a day that would stay with me for a long time to come.

* * *

As soon as I stepped through the front door, the phone rang. Startled, I set the grocery bags on the kitchen counter and rushed across the room, snagging the phone off its cradle just as it began its fifth ring.

"Hello?" I gasped into the receiver.

Static crackled in my ear before a voice cut through. "Sara, it's Clara Sutton. How are you, hon?"

"Fine, just fine, Clara," I replied. "Thanks for asking. And yourself?"

"Right as rain. Listen, I have a favor to ask. It's my niece, Ellie, the one from Ohio. She's spending the summer with me, and her mother insists on her having an algebra tutor. Naturally, I thought of you. I know it's last minute, but do you think you could spare some time?"

I hesitated, thinking about my plans with Jack. "Clara, I'd love to. It's just..."

"It would only be for a few hours in the mornings, and I'll pay you for your time."

I thought it over, considering how the extra income would come in handy. "How old is Ellie?"

"She's your age. She just finished her first year of college at Indiana University."

Something akin to curiosity, or perhaps it was intuition, stirred within me. "I see," I said, mulling over Clara's request. "All right, Clara. I think I can make it work."

"Wonderful. I knew I could count on you. And who knows, you and Ellie might even become good friends."

As soon as I hung up with Clara, I called Jack at the dock. "Hey," I said as soon as he picked up. "I've got some news."

"Good or bad?"

"I'm not sure yet." I hesitated, my fingers absentmindedly twirling around the phone cord. "Remember how I said I might help you and George out this summer? Well, it turns out Clara's niece is staying with her for a few months, and she needs someone to help her with algebra, so I told her I'd do it."

"You mean Ellie?"

"Yes. How did you know?"

Jack chuckled lightly. "Small town. News spreads fast."

"Oh. But it's only for a few hours in the mornings, so we can still fish in the evenings."

"That's fine by me," said Jack. "Plus, I'm sure Ellie could use a friend. It can't be easy being that far from home."

My anxiety dissolved with Jack's understanding. "Thanks, Jack. You're the best."

"Don't mention it."

* * *

The next morning, I arrived at Clara's doorstep just as the sun topped the mountains. Clara welcomed me with her usual warmth and led me to the living room where Ellie was already seated by the window with a pile of books spread out before her.

"Morning, Ellie," I said, offering her a friendly smile. "I'm Sara."

She looked up from her books, her striking brown eyes wide with curiosity, and extended her hand. "Nice to meet you, Sara."

Her accent, coupled with her contemporary fashion—a light blue shirtwaist dress with three-quarter sleeves, paired with cream-colored lace ankle socks and while buckled shoes—gave away her Northern roots. Not to mention she was undeniably beautiful. Still, I had hopes that beneath her polished exterior that she was just another girl in need of guidance and companionship.

"Clara mentioned that you're a math major at the University of Tennessee," Ellie began. "That's impressive. I happen to be studying astronomy myself."

"Really? That's so interesting! I'm curious by nature, so I've always found the stars fascinating—the mystery, the vastness, the beauty. I guess it's the mathematician in me, but my focus has been on the numbers behind it all. How they come together to create this cohesive universe."

Ellie chuckled, her eyes sparkling with amusement. "The cosmos is a magnificent combination of numbers and light, an eternal performance of physics and wonder. I suppose that makes us both seekers in our own way, doesn't it?"

I nodded in agreement. "Clara says you're needing some help with algebra. Is that right?"

Her smile faltered slightly. "Maybe just a refresher. I got an A-minus this semester, which isn't bad, but apparently not good enough for my mother."

"I know what you mean. My mother is always on me about one thing or another."

Ellie laughed at that.

"But don't worry. We'll get you up to an 'A' in no time. And who knows, maybe you'll end up teaching me a thing or two about the stars."

CHAPTER 10

The next evening, I took the path from my house to the dock, hoping to find Jack. Between my chores and helping Ellie, I'd had a full day, so I was ready to kick back and relax. But as I topped the hill, I noticed Jack talking to someone. I squinted against the setting sun, trying to make out the figure. The laughter between them floated across the dock like a bird in flight, settling around me, making my stomach twist in knots. As I drew closer, I realized that the person Jack was talking to was none other than Ellie. I stood frozen for a moment, my mind racing, trying to piece together what was happening.

Their silhouettes, framed against the crimson sunset, seemed to dance in my vision. Jack was leaning back on his hands, while Ellie, with her dainty figure and brown curls, rested against the rail. I could see her full cheeks dimpled in laughter from where I stood.

Jack, with his tanned skin and messy hair, glanced at her, his eyes full of adoration. Something akin to a stone dropped heavily into my stomach. The sight of them together struck an unexpected note of jealousy in my heart. But I couldn't help staring at the scene that had forcefully presented itself to me. Ellie's head tilted back in laughter, her hand lightly touching Jack's arm, and he looked at her as if she were the only star in his sky.

I watched helplessly as they got into the boat, and Jack

started the motor. Part of me wanted to shout out, to make my presence known, but another part held me back. It was a powerful restraint, binding me to the shadows as I watched Ellie and him glide away over the rippling water, their laughter carried away by the cool evening breeze. And it was at that moment I felt a pang of loss that I couldn't quite explain.

Bewildered and hurt, I raced home, retracing my steps along the dirt path now blanketed by evening's shadows. Over the years, I had gotten used to being Jack's fishing partner, the one who shared his laughter and amusing stories as we killed time waiting for bites on our lines. Seeing Ellie in my spot, wearing the spare life vest I usually donned, was disconcerting. It wasn't just about fishing or the seat in the boat. It felt like Ellie had taken advantage of our burgeoning friendship and inserted herself into my place in Jack's life.

"Home so soon?" Mother called from the kitchen as I burst through the front door. "I thought you were going fishing with Jack."

"I thought so, too." I stood in the doorway, watching as she deftly kneaded dough for chicken and dumplings. The warm, inviting smells of home no longer brought me solace. Instead, they seemed to underline the rapid shift in my world.

"Something wrong?" she asked, glancing over her shoulder at me.

I shook my head and forced a smile. "Jack had something come up last minute."

Before she could respond, I went to my room and sank down onto my bed. My mind was filled with thoughts of Jack and Ellie, their laughter echoing in my ears. Despite telling myself I could be happy only being friends with Jack, it was becoming clear that the reality was far more complex. Perhaps in some unspoken corner of my heart, I had been harboring feelings for him that had remained dormant until now.

The world seemed to be closing in on me. The hoots from an owl in a distant tree, the whispered rustling of leaves outside my window, everything just seemed to amplify the gnawing emptiness within me. I rolled onto my side, my gaze falling on the framed photo on my bedside table. It was a picture of Jack and me, taken last summer at the county fair. We were both smiling, cotton candy clutched in our hands, the Ferris wheel a joyful blur behind us.

In that picture, Jack was mine. He wore the same lopsided grin I adored, his eyes lighting up the way they only did when we were together. The memory of that day was so vivid—the sugary sweetness of the cotton candy lingering on my tongue, the warmth of the midday sun on my shoulders, our laughter as we competed in the potato sack race. I remembered how he reached out to wipe a blob of cotton candy off my nose, his fingers lingering just a moment too long. There had been a thrill in that touch, which I took as an unspoken promise.

Now that felt like a distant dream, a mirage of a perfect friendship that was beginning to fade and warp as reality set in. I couldn't reconcile the Jack in my memories with the young man who now rode around with Ellie. Feeling as if the floor had dropped out from under me, I let the picture frame slip from my fingers. It landed with a muted thump on the soft quilt, echoing the heaviness in my heart. I closed my eyes, trying to block out the smiling faces that seemed to mock me from within their wooden frame, but it was no use. The damage had been done.

Present

"In retrospect, I should have approached both Jack and Ellie with an open heart and tried to be friendly, but I didn't. Believe it or not, I wanted more than anything for Ellie and I to be friends. I wanted to show her that I too was someone she could trust and rely on, and that she could rely on me. But every time I thought about reaching out, jealousy would rear its ugly head, reminding me of what I had lost and what I could never have. So I bottled everything up, locking it away in the deepest corners of my heart, hoping that time would wash it away like the ocean does to footprints in the sand. But just like the ocean, time was indifferent to my plight."

Diane studied me for a moment, the muscles around her eyes relaxing a bit. "Perhaps we should take a little break."

We rose from our chairs and made our way outside. The afternoon was unusually mild, reminding me of fall days back home.

We strolled along the edge of the garden, Diane beside me. I felt her gaze on me every now and then but didn't turn to meet it. Instead, my eyes were drawn to the blooms that dotted the landscape. Pops of red, purple, and yellow contrasted beautifully with the lush green of the garden.

"I wish I could tell you things got better after that, but the truth is they only got worse. Sadly, most of it was my own doing. I let my jealousy fester, turning it into destructive force that would not stop until it had consumed everything in its path." I chuckled, thinking how misguided I had been in those days. "And to think, I had convinced myself that Ellie was the storm. But in reality I was the tempest. All Ellie ever did was fall in love, and I punished her for it. Jack, too."

Diane nodded thoughtfully, her eyes flicking to me and then back to the pathway. "Unfortunately, I've crossed paths with a few Ellies in my time. It's hard, isn't it? To watch someone you care about fall in love with someone else?"

"It was like watching a car crash in slow motion. I wanted to look away, but I couldn't. I was so caught up in my own misery that I couldn't see the happiness they found in each other. I became the monster in their love story, shadowing their joy with my bitterness."

We walked down to the beach and took off our shoes, letting the sand seep between our toes. I looked out at the ocean and took a deep breath, tasting the salt on my lips. While Diane kicked at the water's edge, I stared silently into the murky water.

"Love has a funny way of blinding us, doesn't it?" Diane said, folding her arms over her chest.

"Yes, it does. And when we finally see the reality of the situation, most often it's too late. But losing my best friend to Ellie was the most painful awakening I've ever experienced. I didn't lose Jack physically, but in every other sense, he was gone. And it wasn't as if I had time to prepare. One minute, we were going along fine, and the next, it was over. It took me a long time to get over that."

"But you did get over it, didn't you?"

I considered that, thinking that perhaps "over" wasn't the right word. Life had simply moved around it, like water flowing over a stone. "Yes," I finally answered. "In a way. But it's more like you learn to live with it. That empty space...doesn't go away. It just becomes part of you."

CHAPTER 11

After a quick bite to eat, the interview resumed. I'd already revealed to Diane how Ellie had swept into town and stolen Jack's heart, but there was more to the tale than just an ill-fated love story. So much more.

I took a moment to gather my thoughts, letting the silence stretch out comfortably between us. Diane looked at me expectantly, her pen at the ready, as if she sensed the climax was on the horizon.

"Once I realized that Jack and Ellie were more than just friends, I decided to intervene. It's something that to this day I still regret, but at the time, it seemed like my only option. My heart belonged to Jack, and watching Ellie become the object of his desire was a pain I couldn't bear. I knew there would be consequences, possibly devastating ones, but the thought of losing Jack forever hurt even more."

Sims Chapel, TN

June 1950

A few days after I had seen Jack and Ellie at the dock together, I was finishing up some chores when the phone rang. It was Connie, calling to tell me she and Yvonne had run into Jack earlier that afternoon.

"And he was getting into George's truck with some girl," she said, her voice ripe with gossip.

"Some girl, huh?" My insides churned. "Who was she?"

"I don't know. I didn't recognize her, but she was really pretty. It must have been Clara's niece, the one you were telling me about."

Of course, I thought bitterly. It had to be her. "Yes," I forced myself to say calmly. "I'm sure that's who it was." The line between us crackled with tension. I drummed my fingers on the kitchen counter, images of Jack and Ellie flitting through my mind, each more painful than the last. "Do you know what they were doing?" I finally mustered the courage to ask, forcing down the lump forming in my throat.

"I don't know. Just riding around, I guess."

My heart pounded against my ribcage, each beat echoing the fears I dared not voice.

"Anyway, I thought you should know," Connie added. "Considering..."

I managed a weak "thank you" before hanging up the phone.

Even after seeing them together at the dock, part of me still held on to the belief that perhaps it was merely a chance encounter. But now it had happened multiple times, and my friends had seen it, so I couldn't ignore it any longer. The image of Jack's loving smile reflected in Ellie's shining eyes haunted me, gnawing at my sanity like a persistent itch I couldn't scratch. "Oh, Jack," I whispered, shaking my head in disbelief. "What are you doing?"

Over the next few weeks, I tried not to think about Jack and Ellie. I tended to my chores, spent time with Connie and

Yvonne, and even started reading again, something I hadn't done since school let out. But no matter where I went, whispers of Jack's new flame followed me. To make matters worse, I was Ellie's tutor, so I had to face her almost every day. Each meeting felt like a stab to my heart, but I swallowed down the bitterness, forced a smile, and carried on with the lessons.

Every now and then, Ellie would speak of Jack—probing in that innocent, casual way of hers, unknowingly twisting the knife deeper into my heart. I tried to maintain my composure, to keep my feelings hidden behind a mask of friendly concern. After all, I couldn't let Ellie see the war that was raging inside me.

Nights were the hardest. Lying alone in my bed, unable to escape my thoughts, the suffocating silence only amplifying the betrayal. I stared up at the ceiling, my eyes tracing the familiar patterns of the stucco as I fought back tears. But despite everything that had happened, I was determined not to let this ruin me. I was stronger than this, and I knew I had to endure.

One warm July morning, I walked to Clara's, using the time alone to ponder if today was the day I would confront Ellie. For weeks, I had been building a fortress of courage, brick by brick, and today, as the rays of the sun gently kissed my face, it felt solid and steady. The realization that she and Jack were together had been a bitter pill to swallow, but I was determined not to let it poison me. I took a deep breath and opened the door, the chimes above announcing my arrival.

"Mornin', Sara," Clara greeted me warmly as I entered.

My eyes were already scanning the room for Ellie. There she was, sitting cross-legged on the sofa, engrossed in a book.

"Morning," I returned the greeting with a weak smile before making my way toward Ellie. With every step, my heart pounded louder in my chest. I had rehearsed this conversation so many times in my head, yet now all the words seemed to have abandoned me.

"Hi, Sara," Ellie said, not taking her eyes off the book. Her tone was casual, as if we were discussing the weather and not a momentous shift in our dynamic. I forced a smile, swallowed my nerves, and sat down next to Ellie on the sofa.

"Hello," I replied, trying to match the casual air she exuded. I glanced at her book, tapping my fingers restlessly on my knee. "Are you ready to get started?"

"Do you mind if I finish this chapter first? I meant to do it yesterday, but I was out late last night. There's some cobbler in the kitchen if you'd like to have some before we get started."

My eye twitched at the mention of the previous night, but I nodded, smoothing my hair behind my ear. "Sure," I said, rising to my feet. I made my way to the kitchen, letting the familiar scent of Clara's famous cobbler fill my senses.

As I entered the kitchen, I paused, glancing back at Ellie who was still absorbed in her book.

"Can I get you a piece of cobbler?" Clara asked. She was leaning against the counter, sipping her morning coffee.

"No. I mean, no thank you. I ate before I left the house. But," I said, dropping my voice to a whisper, "perhaps there's something else you could help me with. I was wondering if you've seen Jack lately."

"Can't say that I have. Why do you ask?"

I hesitated, gnawing my lower lip thoughtfully. "I just... He's been so busy lately, I haven't seen hide nor hair of him. Which is unlike Jack."

Clara's eyes widened slightly, her coffee mug paused midway to her lips. "I know George has been keeping him busy at the dock."

"Yeah, I'm sure that's it."

"Ready when you are," Ellie announced as she closed her book and set it aside on the coffee table.

For two hours, I quizzed Ellie on inequalities, functions, and polynomials. The numbers and patterns consumed her, providing a temporary relief from the gnawing concerns I had about her burgeoning relationship with Jack.

When we were all done, we ate lunch and spent some time on the back porch, watching the squirrels and listening to the birds sing in the trees.

"Are you enjoying your summer?" I asked, attempting small talk.

"So far," said Ellie. "By the way, thank you for doing this. I'm sure there are a hundred things you'd rather be doing this summer besides helping me study."

"Think nothing of it. Besides, Clara is paying me, so it isn't all bad. How are you keeping yourself busy in the afternoons?"

For a second, I thought I saw a hint of blush in her cheeks, as if she was hiding a secret. "Oh, you know, this and that. Clara's taken me to Dandridge a few times and to Knoxville, but mostly I piddle around here."

I couldn't help myself and probed deeper. "Have you been on the water yet?"

Ellie looked up sharply, perhaps sensing that I knew more than I was letting on. "A couple of times."

"I may have told you, but Jack works down at the dock. If you're interested, maybe we could all go fishing sometime?"

"Um, yeah, maybe. So you and Jack are close?" Ellie asked.

"Close as two friends can be. We've known each other since we were old enough to walk. I reckon he knows the water about as good as anyone around here. Says he wants to own his own business someday."

She leaned in, a mischievous smile gracing her lips. "You and Jack ever, you know...?"

The directness of her question caught me off guard. Almost instantly, I could feel my face heat. "Heavens, no. Well, I take that back. He did kiss me last summer," I said, embellishing the truth just a bit. "But I sort of got the impression he didn't like it much. He only did it once. I don't take it personal though. Jack's a bachelor, and I suspect he always will be."

"What makes you say that?"

"Jack's heart belongs to the water, always has, and probably always will. I'm not saying it's impossible, but I reckon it'd take a special girl to tear him away from it."

While Ellie turned and stared out the window, I thought about what I had said. It was true, Jack loved the water. But he also valued friendship and loyalty, both of which I offered him in abundance. And for the first time since learning of Jack and Ellie's escapades on the water, I was hopeful that in time this storm would pass.

* * *

A few days later, I was finishing up Ellie's lesson when I saw Jack coming up the path to Clara's house.

"Jack." I stepped out onto the porch, flashing a grin. "What are you doing here?"

"Oh hey, Sara. Long time no see. I came by to talk to Ellie."

The disappointment nearly knocked me over, but I hid it well behind a practiced smile. "Oh. I've been meaning to congratulate you on catching that lunker a while back. George told me all about it."

"Thanks, but I didn't catch it. Ellie did. First cast, too."

My smile wavered just a tad at that. "Is that so? I didn't realize she knew how to fish."

"She didn't until I taught her."

"How nice of you. Maybe you could show me where you caught it sometime. I've been dying to get out on the water."

"You know the place," Jack said matter-of-factly. "It's up at the head of Muddy Creek, near the bridge. I took you there last summer, remember?"

I frowned, recalling the day. It had been hot, so hot that even the water had been warm to the touch. We spent the day basking in the sun, lazily casting our lines. It didn't matter that we hadn't caught anything because I had Jack, and that was enough for me. "Oh yeah. Must have forgot."

When Ellie appeared, I slipped away and took the path that led into the woods. There, I found a quiet spot beneath the oak tree where Jack and I had carved our names as kids. It was a sacred spot, a place where we used to escape the world and all its trouble. The engraved letters, now faded by the elements, brought a bitter taste to my mouth.

I sat for hours, listening to the creek and watching the shadows stretch and retreat as the sun moved across the sky. Despite my best efforts, my thoughts wandered back to Jack. What were he and Ellie doing right now? Were they laughing, telling jokes, listening to music on the radio the way we used to? Or were they walking hand in hand, lost in the kind of intimacy we never had?

A soft breeze rustled through the leaves, whispering secrets of its own. I closed my eyes, letting the sound wash over me as I sank deeper into my thoughts. It was hard to believe that Jack— my Jack—was now Ellie's. The thought of them together was overwhelming, leaving me breathless and broken.

CHAPTER 12

By the time August arrived, I had reached my wits end. Most days, Jack was busy at the dock. But occasionally, he'd come to Clara's, offering a helping hand with the chores or simply looking for an excuse to be near Ellie. Watching them exchange glances when they thought I wasn't looking, knowing they were constantly slipping away to do God knows what, was like a slow death. I tried not to let it get to me, but they were always there, in the corner of my eye, a constant reminder of what I had lost.

Still, I knew that the end of summer meant the end of their summer fling. Ellie would be returning to Ohio soon, and Jack was headed to Knoxville to begin work at the factory. The thought gave me cruel comfort, a small reprieve from the heartache that had, for months, consumed me.

Eager to try and salvage my friendship with Jack, I decided to make a bold move.

"Hey, you," I said, finding him sitting at the end of the dock one hot August evening, shoes off, feet in the water.

"Hey," he responded without looking at me. His voice was flat, devoid of the usual warmth that used to make my heart flutter.

I took a deep breath, bracing myself for the impending awkwardness. "We need to talk, Jack."

"I figured we would sooner or later."

I took a cautious step forward, then another, until I was

close enough to sit next to him. The night was quiet, the moon casting long shadows over the water. "You and Ellie..." I began, my voice shaky. "I know what's going on. I've seen the way you two look at each other. I know you've been sneaking off together. Why, Jack?" My question came out in a whisper, a plea for an answer I wasn't sure I wanted.

Jack didn't answer right away, his gaze still directed at the water. Finally, he turned toward me, his face illuminated by the moonlight. "Because I love her. That's why."

It was a simple statement, uttered with a sincerity that left no room for doubt.

My heart sank, the words slicing through me like a knife. "I see. And does she love you?"

He hesitated, looking back to the water. "Yes. We are in love with each other."

A pang of agony coursed through me all at once. I felt as if the ground beneath me had given way, my world crumbling around me. I blinked back my tears, resolving not to let him see me break. "Thank you for being honest," I managed to say, each word feeling like shards of glass scraping against my heart. "That's all I wanted."

He frowned, as if he was just now sensing the depth of my pain. "I'm sorry, Sara. I never meant for you to get hurt."

His apology stung, a harsh reminder of the reality I was now forced to live with. But despite the ache gnawing at my heart, I managed a small smile. "I know you didn't."

He stood up then, rising to his feet as the emptiness inside me threatened to swallow me whole. And as he did, something small fell out of his pocket and landed with a soft thud. I glanced at it, and for a moment I didn't want to believe what I was seeing. There, on the wooden planks of the dock, lay a small black box.

It couldn't be, could it? With trembling fingers, I picked it up. It was heavier than I expected, the smooth velvet soft against my skin. Unable to resist, I opened the box and gasped.

Inside was a beautiful diamond ring, the stone glimmering in the moonlight. Immediately, I shut the box, hoping that by doing so I could erase the sight of it. I handed it back to him, my hand shaking slightly.

"Thanks," was all he said as he took the box and slipped it back into his pocket.

The silence that followed was heavy. Jack kept looking at the ground, a deep crease marking his forehead. "Listen, I—"

"Don't," I said, cutting him off. I didn't want any more excuses or apologies. I didn't want to hear about how he still cared for me. All I wanted was for the pain to stop, for the world to start making sense again. But after what I had seen, I wasn't sure if that would ever be possible.

He took a step back, turned, and started to walk away. But after a few steps, he paused. "I am sorry, Sara. Truly, I am."

I watched him go, the cool breeze brushing against my cheeks and tangling my hair. "So am I, Jack," I said as he faded into the night. "So am I."

Present

The chime of the grandfather clock in the study pulled me back to the present. I looked at Diane, who had tears in her eyes.

"At the time, it was the worst moment of my life," I said, fighting back tears of my own.

"It's hard to imagine a woman as strong as you ever being heartbroken," said Diane.

I gave her a small smile, appreciating the sentiment. "Strength often comes from heartbreak. It's not something you're born with. It's something you learn. And believe me, I've learned a lot over the years."

When Diane composed herself, she asked, "So, what happened next? Did Jack propose to Ellie? Did she say yes?"

"He was going to," I answered as I took a deep breath. "But things didn't go quite as planned."

Sims Chapel, TN

August 1950

After seeing the engagement ring, I didn't know what to do. I couldn't bear the thought of Jack proposing to Ellie, or her saying yes. Despite everything, I was still deeply in love with him. Out of time and options, I decided not to leave this in the hands of fate. If I wanted Jack, I had to fight for him. So, I did the unthinkable.

* * *

When the sun came up the next morning, I went straight to Clara's to pick up a notebook I had left. Thankfully, Ellie wasn't home.

"Mornin', Sara," Clara said opening the door for me. "Won't you come in?"

Part of me wanted to tell Clara about Jack's plan to propose to Ellie, but I knew better. Clara adored Jack, and Ellie was her niece, so the odds of her being on my side were slim. I decided to keep it to myself.

Instead, as we searched for the notebook, I happened to stumble upon Clara's address book, which contained the number for Marie Spencer, Ellie's mother. Acting on impulse, I jotted down the number and left the house with a hollow goodbye.

* * *

The phone was cold in my hands as I dialed Marie's number that evening, my heart pounding against my ribs. When she answered, I introduced myself and divulged to her the details of Jack's plan. Naturally, she was horrified. After all, Ellie was only nineteen, and with a promising career ahead of her, she was far too young to be tied down by marriage. Before we hung up, Marie thanked me for the information and promised to handle the situation.

The following day crept by, the minutes feeling like hours as I waited to see what Marie would do. After dinner, I took the path to Clara's house and waited at the edge of the woods. The sun had nearly set when I finally saw Marie's car pull into the driveway. I took a deep breath, my heart in my throat. As soon as she stepped out of the vehicle, I could see she was angry. Her face was hardened, her eyes filled with determination as she marched toward the house. She paused by the front door, straightening her shoulders before ringing the bell. Clara soon answered, her face dropping at the sight of her sister. I couldn't hear their conversation, but from the look on Clara's face, it was quite serious.

After a few minutes, Marie reappeared with Ellie trailing close behind. Ellie's face was a mask of confusion as she looked from Clara to her mother, clearly taken aback by the unexpected visit. Marie led Ellie quickly to the car and soon they drove away.

I felt a pang of guilt watching Ellie's receding figure through the car's back window. She looked lost, her eyes wide with uncertainty. She turned back toward Clara's house, and for a moment, I thought she saw me. I quickly stepped back into the shadows, hoping she hadn't.

Later that night, I went in search of Jack. I found him sitting on his back porch, shoulders slumped in defeat. "What's the matter?" I asked as I eased toward him.

He looked up and wiped tears from his eyes as he tucked something into his pocket. "She's gone," he said, lifting his gaze to the full moon. "Ellie's gone."

I sat beside him, feeling a mix of relief and regret. "I'm sorry, Jack. I know how much you liked her."

"The worst part is I never even got to ask her to marry me."

Seeing Jack this way, in utter despair, broke my heart. But at least he wasn't engaged. That would have shattered my heart into a million irreparable pieces.

"Is there anything I can do?"

He shook his head. "There's nothing anyone can do now."

"Did she say why she left?" I knew it was terrible of me to ask, but I had to know.

Jack fumbled to retrieve the crumpled letter from his pocket and handed it to me. I stared at it, regret bubbling up inside me. When I finished reading, I didn't know what to say. I reached out and touched Jack's arm. He didn't pull away, but neither did he acknowledge my touch. It was as though I had become invisible to him.

"Maybe it's for the best. I know it might be hard to see now, but in time you might feel differently."

Jack looked at me then, and I could see the pain swimming

in his tear-filled eyes. "For the best? God, Sara, you don't get it, do you? Do you really think Ellie means so little to me that I could just move on?"

I flinched at his words, my heart aching for him and breaking at the same time. "I didn't mean it like that. I just meant—"

"You meant well, I know." Jack cut me off, his lips pressed into a tight line. "But it's just... It's not that simple."

I nodded, understanding even if I didn't want to. I wished I could take his pain away, wished I could be the one to make him smile again. But as I sat there, a series of unsaid emotions dancing between us, I realized my feelings for Jack were far more profound than I had dared to admit initially. I loved him, I realized, with a love as vast and endless as the star-studded sky above us. And it was that quiet, painful acknowledgment that had me wishing that Ellie Spencer had never come into our lives.

I felt a swell of longing for simpler times, when the love I had for Jack was pure, before my heart was broken, before I resorted to treachery to get another chance at his heart.

This summer had changed me, and I wondered if things would ever be the same again.

CHAPTER 13

Present

When I finished telling the story, Diane looked at me with a mixture of shock and understanding. I could tell she was searching for the right words, unsure of what to say.

"Wow," she finally said. "That's not what I was expecting."

"I know. It wasn't my finest moment, but it's what happened."

Diane took off her glasses and leaned back, clearing her throat. "I can't say that I agree with what you did, but I understand why you did it. Love can make us do crazy things."

The bitter laugh that escaped my lips seemed to surprise us both. "Crazy doesn't even begin to cover it." I stared into the fire, the flames dancing as memories of that summer played out in my mind. The betrayal, the secrets, and the lies. "I wish I could take it all back," I whispered, more to myself than to Diane. "It's the single biggest regret of my life."

After Diane had scribbled a few notes on her pad, I heard the click of the recorder. "I think that's enough for today." Perhaps she sensed that I had delved as far into my past as I could handle for one afternoon. Or maybe she saw the raw vulnerability in my eyes and decided it best not to push me further. Either way, the silence that followed was a welcome reprieve from the torment of my confession.

* * *

That evening, I ate alone. The food was flavorless, each bite a reminder of the emptiness growing inside me. I stared out the window at the setting sun, its fiery glow matching the flames I had poured my heart out to earlier. I thought about Diane and her quiet understanding. She was a good listener, but there was only so much she could do.

I barely noticed when Judy came to clear away the untouched food from my tray.

"Rough day?"

"You could say that."

"I heard you mention Jack this afternoon," she said, placing the dishes in the sink. "You haven't talked about him in years. Are you sure this was a good idea?"

I shrugged, my eyes fixed on the table. "I don't know, Judy. Part of me thought that telling my story would be therapeutic. But another part... Anyway, I think the worst is behind me. Diane now knows what only a handful of people know—that I betrayed Jack, that I lied to him, and that it was all because of a love that consumed me."

"But why even dredge up all those painful memories? It was so long ago, and you've accomplished so much since then. Besides, what happened that summer doesn't define the woman you are today."

"But it does," I said. "It's like a stain on my soul. No matter how much I've achieved, no matter how much good I've done— it always comes back to that summer."

* * *

As darkness fell, I found myself lost in thought. The ghosts of my past seemed to be hovering in the room, their cold fingers brushing against my heart. Whenever I closed my eyes, I saw Jack's face, his blue eyes, the curve of his jaw, the way his lips turned up in a smile whenever he saw me. I could feel the warmth of his embrace, the tender kisses he used to press against my forehead. He was a part of me, a part that I had tried so hard to bury and forget.

Wednesday

The next morning, I began my day by penning an entry in my journal. I started the ritual years ago, having been inspired by Jack. I found writing cathartic, a way to drain the poison from my soul, one word at a time. I was no novelist, but I wrote with the raw honesty of someone who had nothing left to lose. My words were my confessions, my repentance, my redemption.

As dawn broke, I readied myself for the day. I slipped into my clothes, the soft cashmere hugging my aged body. The ritual of applying makeup was soothing, the brush against the skin, the delicate balance of color and light that accentuated my eyes and gave my cheeks a rosy hue.

The mirror reflected a woman of strength and wisdom, someone who had earned every line on her face, every strand of silver in her hair. I stared at the reflection for a long time, seeing not only the woman I had become, but also the young girl from so long ago. Her innocence lost, her heart shattered. But her spirit remained unbroken.

* * *

After breakfast, I made my way into the library, where Diane was already waiting.

"I hope you don't mind, but I wanted to get an early start on the day. I feel as if we still have much to talk about."

Yes, I thought. There was much more to say, many more memories to dig up from the graveyard of my past. "I don't mind at all," I responded warmly, feeling recharged and ready. "In fact, I'm eager too."

With that, we settled into our familiar positions, with her opposite me, a notebook in her lap and an expectant look on her face. Once the tape recorder was set, I began to tell her about what happened in the weeks and months following my betrayal.

Sims Chapel, TN

August 1950

The moment Ellie left Sims Chapel, an overwhelming sense of relief washed over me. It was like the weight of the world had suddenly been lifted from my shoulders. But with the start of my sophomore year of college only days away, the relief was short-lived.

Complicating matters was the fact that my two closest friends, Connie and Yvonne, who had always been there to provide me comfort and support, were leaving for their own respective colleges soon. In a matter of days, we'd all be scattered across the state again, each of us picking up where we'd left off the previous spring.

"I, for one, can't wait to get back to Nashville," Connie declared during our last get-together at her house. "I mean, don't get me wrong, I love y'all, but Sims Chapel is just so small.

So stifling."

Yvonne nodded sympathetically as she sipped her sweet tea. "I feel the same way about Clarksville. But I believe it's the change of scenery that does us good. Don't you, Sara?"

Before I could answer, Connie chimed in. "You're just excited to be closer to that boy you met last spring. Don't deny it, Yvonne!"

Yvonne blushed a deep scarlet. "Speaking of boys..." She turned to me. "What's the story with Jack and old what's-her-name?"

My heart clenched. "They're still together, if that's what you mean. But time and distance will take care of that. And when it does, I'll be waiting."

"Don't you think that maybe it's time you gave up on that dream?" Connie suggested. "I mean, there are so many other fish in the sea besides Jack Bennett. You're a gorgeous girl, Sara, and smart as a whip. How 'bout you set your sights on some of those college boys you were telling us about?"

I smiled, thinking of the prospect. There had been one or two boys the previous year who had tried to catch my attention. Good looking boys, intelligent, too. But my heart still yearned for Jack. "Maybe," I mused, "but I can't imagine any of them measuring up to him."

Yvonne shook her head, a sorrowful look in her eyes. "Sara, I fear your heart might be too set on him. It's not healthy pining for someone who's taken."

"Perhaps," I conceded, staring at the ice in my glass. "But it's not like I can switch my feelings off." I looked up to see Connie and Yvonne exchange glances before Yvonne reached out and squeezed my hand.

"Sweetie," she said, "sometimes, we don't get the things we

want the most. And that's okay. It hurts, but it often leads us to something better."

Connie nodded, her expression serious. "And sometimes, what we think we want isn't really what's best for us. We have to trust that life has better plans."

I laughed, the sound a little bitter. "And what if life doesn't know best? What if we know better?"

Yvonne's gaze was steady. "Then we fight for it, Sara. But just be sure it's worth fighting for. Otherwise, you might end up losing something even more precious in the process."

Despite my friends' advice, I felt a sense of determination that wasn't there before. I was going to have Jack, no matter what it took. I would win him over, make him see that I was the one he should be with, not Ellie. The foolish thought was born out of naivety and stubbornness, but it was all I had. And I clung to it like a lifeline.

To my disappointment, the weeks and months following Ellie's departure bore no fruit. Even with her hundreds of miles away, Jack seemed more in love with her than ever. I even heard he took a bus to visit her in Bloomington, utterly defeating my hopes of his affection waning with distance. It was then that I finally started to accept the truth: I had been chasing a fantasy, a figment of my imagination, and my turn with Jack would never come. So I slowly began to let go, allowing the remnants of my dream to trickle away. I still had moments of weakness, of longing, but I tried my best to suppress them. But before I could completely sever my feelings for Jack, fate stepped in once again.

Sims Chapel, TN

November 1950

I returned home to celebrate the Thanksgiving holiday with my mother, who had prepared a spread so large it was as if she was expecting the entire town to drop by. There was the usual turkey, dressing, green bean casserole, sweet potato pie with marshmallows, and a multitude of colorful vegetables scattered across the countertop. I tried to tell her it was too much food, but she merely waved me off, insisting that there was no such thing as too much on Thanksgiving.

After a hearty meal, I was clearing the table when she asked if I could take some leftovers to George.

"I promised him some turkey and dressing, and a piece of my sweet potato pie," Mother said as she packed a picnic basket with generous portions of food.

"Of course," I said, dreading the thought of going out into the cold but unable to refuse her request.

Bundled up in my coat, gloves, and boots, I hiked through the woods to deliver the meal to George. When I got there, I found his cabin empty, the door swung wide. Concerned, I poked my head inside, calling out his name.

"George?"

"No, just me," came a familiar voice.

I stepped into the kitchen and was surprised to find Jack there, hunched over a wooden table, nursing a glass of sweet tea. His face was a picture of gloom, his eyes sad and rimmed with red. The sight of him, so desolate and vulnerable, sent a pang through my heart.

"Jack? What are you doing here?" I asked as I shut the door

behind me. "And where's George?"

Jack looked up at me, his eyes dull and lost. "He's out getting more wood... Said he'd be back soon," he said, gesturing toward the dwindling fire. "I just needed a place to clear my head."

I set the basket down on the table and grabbed a chair to sit on. "Why the long face? Is everything okay?"

He shrugged, his gaze drifting back to the half-empty glass in front of him. "Not really."

"Do you want to talk about it?"

Jack hesitated. "I don't know if that's such a good idea."

"Oh," I said, putting two and two together. "It's about her, isn't it?"

He nodded, his expression turning even more grim.

"Whatever it is, I'm sure you'll get through it," I said, trying to take the high road.

"But that's just it... I don't know if we will this time. You see, I made a fool of myself in front of her friends...let my temper get the best of me...again. Anyway, I ended up leaving a day early and we haven't spoken since."

I stared at Jack, unsure of what to say. He was usually so cheerful, so full of life. Seeing him defeated was disturbing. "Did you try apologizing?" I asked hesitantly, unsure of whether I was crossing a line.

"Of course I did. But she didn't want to hear it... Said it was probably best if we took a break. I don't know, Sara. It's like Ellie's a different person when she's around her friends... Like I don't recognize her at all."

I couldn't believe my ears. All this time I had been searching for an opportunity to prove to Jack that Ellie was the wrong girl for him, that he deserved someone who understood him, someone better. Someone like me. But instead of reveling in this moment, I felt a deep sense of sorrow seeing him in such a state.

"Ellie's probably just trying to fit in," I suggested, masking the surge of hope that was bubbling inside me. "People sometimes act differently when they're around other people."

Jack looked up at me and managed a half-hearted smile. "You think?"

"Yeah, I do. We all have different sides, Jack. It doesn't mean she doesn't still…" I wanted to say love, but the word got caught in my throat. "It doesn't mean she doesn't still care about you."

"Maybe you're right."

"Of course I'm right," I said, then went about unpacking the basket I had brought for George. "Have you eaten yet?"

"I had a little something earlier, but I could eat."

"Well, there's enough in here for the both of you," I said, revealing turkey legs, rolls, and sweet potato pie among other things. "When George gets back, you both can eat to your heart's delight."

He managed a larger smile this time, a small slice of the old Jack I knew making its way through the gloom. "Thanks, Sara. You always know how to cheer me up."

His words warmed my heart. "It's what friends do, right?" I said, trying to keep my voice steady. I couldn't show him how much those words meant to me.

"Right. Hey, Sara?"

"Yes?"

"Thank you, for everything. You really are a good friend."

I swallowed hard, fighting the lump in my throat. "You're welcome. And remember, if you ever need someone to talk to, I'm always here."

I left the cabin that evening with a bittersweet taste in my mouth. I had fought the urge to tell Jack how I truly felt, that he should forget about Ellie and be with me instead. But I couldn't betray his trust like that, not when he was so vulnerable and lost. I could only shoulder his burdens and remain by his side, a loyal friend, even if my heart yearned for more.

CHAPTER 14

Over the course of the next couple of months, I kept my distance from Jack, focusing all of my time and energy on school and my part-time job at the campus library. Jack had always been my closest friend, but the feelings I had for him, unreciprocated and intense, made it impossible to maintain the same level of closeness we once shared.

Fortunately, I met someone—a boy from my anthropology class named Ryan. He was handsome and charming, with a soft-spoken demeanor that was comforting and sincere. We fell into a comfortable rhythm, studying together during the week and going out on casual dates on weekends. For a time, it seemed like I could move on from my complicated feelings for Jack. But then, early one morning, I received a knock on my door that upended everything.

Knoxville, TN

February 1951

Jack didn't say a word when I opened the door, just handed me a letter with trembling hands. He looked even worse than the last time I had seen him. His hollowed-out cheeks made his eyes look bigger and sadder, his unkempt hair showing the stress of a sleepless night.

"Jack, what's happened?" I asked, concerned by his appearance.

He shook his head, slumping onto the couch in my living room. I took a seat beside him, opening the letter. A gasp escaped my lips as I read the words typed on the crisp, official-looking paper. It was a draft notice. Jack was being called to serve in the Korean War. I blinked rapidly, trying to stave off the tears pricking at the corners of my eyes.

"It's going to be okay," I told him, not only trying to convince him, but myself as well. "You're going to be okay."

He looked at me, his eyes glassy. "You don't know that, Sara. No one knows that for sure."

The reality of the situation started to sink in. Jack wasn't just going away for a while. He was going to war. But I couldn't let my fear show. He needed me to be strong for him, even if inside I felt like I was breaking apart.

"You're right. I don't know that for sure. But what I do know is that you're strong. You're brave. And you have a whole lot of people who care about you and will be praying for your safe return." His eyes searched mine, looking for certainty, for reassurance. In that moment, I found a reservoir of strength within myself I didn't know existed. I held his gaze, unblinking, and nodded. "Just promise me you'll be careful. Promise me you won't take any unnecessary risks. You mean too much to me, Jack...to everyone who cares about you."

He stared at me for a long time before he nodded once, slowly. "I promise."

Over the next few weeks, I saw Jack several times. We went for long walks in the woods, sat for hours on the dock, and talked about anything and everything under the sun.

The night before he left, we sat under a sky so clear you could see the Milky Way stretching out above us. Jack turned to me, his face lit by the ghostly glow of the moon. "I need you to do something for me while I'm gone."

"Anything," I said, knowing that I would move mountains for him if he asked.

"I want you to hold onto this." From his coat pocket, he pulled a small leather notebook and handed it to me. "Do you know what this is?"

I nodded, recognizing the cover. "It's your journal...the one you write in every day."

"Guard this with your life."

"Jack, I don't know what to say. Are you sure you don't want to keep this with you?"

He shook his head, his expression solemn. "If anything were to happen to me, I want it returned to Mama. I'd ask her to keep it, but she's upset enough as it is. I just can't stand the thought of it falling into the hands of a stranger, being lost and forgotten."

"All right," I said, biting back tears. "I'll guard it with my life. But Jack, you better not do anything that would make me have to give this back to your Mama." The thought of that was too much for my poor heart to bear.

The next day, I drove Jack to the bus station in Knoxville. Our goodbye was brief and painful, both of us trying to be strong for the other. I waited until he was out of sight before shedding any tears. But as soon as his bus rounded that corner, I collapsed on a nearby bench, my body wracked with sobs. Salty tears streamed down my cheeks, each one carrying a piece of my heart that went away with Jack.

* * *

After that, time moved in slow motion. To distract myself from the pain, I threw myself into schoolwork, studying late into the night until the words blurred on the page and sleep pulled me under its heavy wing. In an attempt to maintain a sense of normalcy, I spent more time with my friends, going to the local diner, the movies, even the occasional dance. I also continued seeing Ryan, though his presence was more of a comfort than anything romantic. Still, being with him made me realize that there was life outside of Jack Bennett, that the world didn't stop turning just because he wasn't around. And for the first time in my life I felt a sense of independence, of self-determination that had been elusive to me until then.

But no matter where I was or what I did, the journal never left my side. I kept it close, treating it as if it were the most precious gem in existence. I didn't dare open it, to invade Jack's inner thoughts and feelings. Its presence, however, was a comforting reminder of him.

In my free time, I wrote letters to Jack, sharing details about my days, about my academic achievement, and snippets of news from our hometown. In return, I received letters from him. His handwriting was hurried, almost unrecognizable, but the words he penned were beautiful and heartbreaking. He wrote of his comrades, the harsh realities of war, and the longing for home. But there was one letter that stood out from all the rest. It arrived in the summer of 1952, a month before the start of my senior year of college.

Dear Sara,

I hope this letter finds you in good health and high spirits. I know it's been a while since I last wrote you, but the fighting has been more relentless than ever. Every day is a battle in itself, not just against the enemy, but also against fear, despair, and the overwhelming longing for home.

Speaking of despair, I received a letter from Ellie last week telling me that she's done with me. I guess she finally got tired of waiting. I can't blame her, though. This war has taken its toll on us all. Anyway, I thought you should know. I also want you to know that your letters are the only thing keeping me going these days. They are a beacon of hope in a seemingly endless night, and I hold onto every word, every stroke of your pen as if it were a lifeline.

There's a tree here, a lone oak standing defiantly amidst the ruin and rubble. I sit under its shade whenever I can steal a moment away from the chaos. It reminds me of the oak tree we used to sit under, the one that has our initials carved into its bark. Do you remember? We were just kids then, wild and free. How things have changed. I miss the innocence of those days, the simplicity that was our childhood. We didn't have a care in the world, just two best friends with dreams bigger than the sky. I'm rambling, aren't I? Sorry, but each time death brushes past me, I find myself retreating into the past, reliving every moment we spent together, just to keep my sanity intact.

But let me tell you something, Sara. Being here in the midst of all this madness, I've come to realize something—life isn't about escaping the storm, it's about learning to dance in the rain. And right now, I am drenched to the bone.

I don't know when I'll be coming home, and the truth is,

*there's a chance I may never get to see you again. If that
happens, I want you to promise me something. Promise me
that you'll remember the boy who used to laugh under the
summer sun and chase dreams in the quiet starlight. Don't
remember me as a soldier lost to the war, but as your friend
who loved life as much as he loved you. Take care of yourself,
Sara, and never let the world dim your beautiful light.*

Yours,

Jack

I don't think I had ever cried as much as I did when
I finished reading that letter. His words seemed to bleed the
pain and longing he had been enduring. Up until then, I had
been hopeful Jack would come back, that the war would end,
and he could pick up where he left off. But his words spoke a
different truth, a fearful possibility that I was too afraid to even
contemplate. Suddenly, his absence felt more real than ever
before. And yet, amidst the despair, a flicker of hope ignited
within me. Jack was free again, no longer tethered to Ellie. And
it wasn't because of some petty act by a lovesick teenager, but
because she had willingly released him.

The old me would have written back immediately, poured
out my feelings and thoughts on paper until there was nothing
left to say. But in the time Jack had been away, I had grown
and matured in ways I never thought possible, my heart no
longer weighed down by the heavy burden of love and longing.
I finally understood what it meant to be independent, to be a
woman not defined by the absence or presence of a man.

Jack's letter, though heavy with desperation and sadness,
had freed me in ways I hadn't anticipated. I was no longer the

girl waiting on the sidelines for him to notice. I was a woman who had learned to stand on her own, to dance in the storm. The words that had once made my heart ache, now fueled my ambition. I was no longer waiting for a hero. I had become my own.

Sims Chapel, TN

April 1953

The day Jack came home was one of the greatest days of my life. Seeing him after all that time was like being plunged into a pool of warm sunlight after enduring a long, harsh winter. He looked different, hardened by war and time. His eyes held a faraway look that spoke volumes about the things he had seen, things he could never unsee. But underneath it all, he was still Jack.

He stepped off the bus, his military uniform crisp and his boots echoing on the pavement. His eyes scanned the crowd waiting at the bus stop, and for a moment he looked lost, as though he was seeing everything here for the first time.

Then, his eyes met mine. The years apart, the letters, the fear, the heartache...all of it collapsed into that one moment.

He broke into a slow smile before he dropped his duffel bag and walked toward me. I ran to meet him halfway, my heart pounding in my chest so hard I thought it might burst. The world seemed to stop spinning for a moment as he swept me into his arms, lifting me off the ground in one swift, powerful motion. I buried my face in the crook of his neck, inhaling his familiar scent.

"I missed you," I said, hardly able to get the words out.

"I missed you, too," he whispered back.

Every worry, every fear, and every sleepless night seemed to melt away in that singular moment of reunion.

We stood there in the midst of the bustling crowd, oblivious to the world around us. He finally set me down but did not let go. Instead, he pulled me closer, wrapping both his arms around me in a protective embrace.

"You're home."

He nodded and took a deep breath. "Yes," he said, his voice rough. "I am."

CHAPTER 15

For a while, all the pieces of my life seemed to be falling into place. A month after Jack returned home, I graduated with a mathematics degree from the University of Tennessee and returned to Sims Chapel, where I took a teaching job at the local high school. With the money I was making, I was able to buy a small place of my own on Deep Springs Road. It was no grand estate, but it was charming, like one of those houses you see on Christmas cards, with a back porch, a little white picket fence, and a small garden in the back.

Life was simple again, just as it had been when I was younger. Waking up early to the crowing of roosters and the smell of dew on the grass, driving to school as the sun peeked over the mountains, and coming home to a quiet house became my daily routine. I even started having lunch with my mother every Sunday after church, a tradition we had abandoned when I went off to college. We'd sit and talk for hours, sipping sweet tea and reminiscing about times gone by. Over the years, our relationship had grown from a mother and daughter to one of close confidantes. She understood my worries, my dreams, my fears, and was always there with a word of wisdom or a comforting shoulder.

And just as the rest of my life settled into a comfortable cadence, Jack and I did as well. On weekends we hiked, fished, and talked about all the changes that had occurred since Jack left. At night, we'd sit on my porch swing, stars twinkling overhead, listening to the chirping of the crickets. We were friends again, back to the same ease we shared as children.

"I'm sorry for all I put you through," Jack said one night, his eyes reflecting the starlight. "With the war, with Ellie, with what happened that summer."

"Water under the bridge," I said softly, leaning into the warmth of his arm around my shoulder.

"I know, but I'd like to make amends. I owe you that."

"You don't owe me anything, Jack. We're past that now."

"But I do. I want to make things right. For you and for us."

A warm breeze caressed my cheeks, carrying with it the hint of rain. I stared into Jack's eyes, a thousand unspoken words hanging between us. "Us?"

"Yes. I don't know why I didn't see it before...or maybe I did and just denied it, but now, I see it clear as day. You're not just my best friend, Sara. You mean more to me than that."

My heart stuttered. Was this it? Was this the moment I had been waiting for all these years? The moment where Jack would finally see me not just as a friend but as something more?

"I care deeply for you, Sara," he said. "And if you're willing to give us another chance, I promise you won't regret it."

My mind was a whirl of thoughts, my heart throbbing in my chest. "Jack, I... I've always cared for you, too, more than you'll ever know. But..." I paused as I searched for the right words. A part of me wanted to throw myself into his arms, to kiss him and let go of all the pent-up emotions I'd been carrying for years. But another part was afraid that giving him more of my heart might only lead to more pain and disappointment. Besides, I had moved on, hadn't I?

As this war raged within me, Jack leaned forward and

kissed me. He pulled back, looking into my eyes with a softness I had never seen before. "Was that okay?" he asked, looking as if he'd done something wrong.

"I... I don't know," was all I could say. "If you'd asked me years ago, the answer would have been a resounding yes. But now..." The truth was, I didn't know what I felt anymore.

"I understand," he said, nodding and turning away. "I had my chances, didn't I? And I squandered them. It's unfair of me to think that after all this time, all the mistakes, I could just swoop in and claim the place in your heart that I so foolishly gave away. But..." He turned back to me, his eyes glistening in the moonlight. "I had to try, Sara. For my own sanity, I had to know if there was even a shred of hope left for us."

"I'm... I'm not so sure, Jack," I stammered, my eyes welling with tears. His words were a balm and a torment, and in that moment, I wished he'd never said them. "I don't know if I can just forget everything...the past...and start anew. It's not so simple."

After a silence that seemed to stretch on for eternity, Jack stood up, his face a stoic mask. "I can't change the past, Sara," he said, his voice deep and full of sorrow. "I can't take back the mistakes I've made, nor can I erase the hurt I've caused. But I can make sure you never have to go through that again." He reached into his pocket and pulled out a silver necklace, a delicate piece I had admired in a shop window years ago. I recalled mentioning it to him casually once, never imagining he would remember. "You don't have to give me an answer now, but if you find it in your heart to give me another chance, I promise things will be different."

His words held a power over me, a magic that made me want to believe. But could I? The scars of the past were still fresh, still raw, keeping me from giving in completely. Nevertheless, I took the necklace from him, hoping that perhaps this time would be different.

* * *

After that night on the porch, we danced around the idea of "us." We continued to meet, sometimes for coffee, other times for walks in the woods. Jack was patient, never pushing, never demanding more than I was willing to give. And with each passing day, I warmed up to him, slowly letting down the walls I'd built around my heart.

Time marched on, and as the deep greens of summer faded to the golds and ambers of fall, so did my resolve. One evening, I found Jack sitting in the cemetery, staring at his brother's headstone. I approached him slowly, the crunch of the fallen leaves under my feet magnified in the stillness of the evening. He did not turn as I neared, his gaze fixed dead ahead.

"I missed you at supper. Is everything all right?"

He didn't answer right away, his gaze unwavering from the black etching on the stone. Tension tightened his jaw. His fists clenched and unclenched sporadically. It was as if he were wrestling with some internal demon, a battle that seemed to consume him entirely.

"Jack?" I dared to ask again, my voice a whisper in the growing darkness. I reached out tentatively, placing my hand on his tense shoulder. He flinched at the contact but didn't pull away.

"I think it's time for me to leave this place." His words fell like stones, sinking heavily into the cool autumn air. I could hear the finality in his tone, the resolution of a decision made after long hours of contemplation.

"Leave? What do you mean?"

He turned toward me, his eyes rimmed red and his face pale. "I mean I need to leave, Sara. Leave this town, these memories...everything."

Though he and I weren't officially together, that moment felt like a punch to the gut. The thought of him leaving again was inconceivable. "Where will you go? What will you do?"

He turned away. "I don't know. I just need time to figure things out, and I can't do it here."

"Then I'll come with you," I said, desperate to keep him from disappearing from my life. "We can go together, Jack. We can figure this out together."

"No, Sara. I can't ask you to do that. You've built a life here, a career. Besides, this isn't your fight."

His words cut me to the core, leaving me exposed. After all this time, he still kept me at arm's length.

"You might think you have to do this alone, Jack, but you don't. You have people here who care for you, who love you. You have your mother, and George, and me."

He attempted to muster a smile, but it came out as more of a grimace. "I know," he uttered, his voice rough with emotion. "You've all shown me that time and time again."

"Then why...? Why do you insist on leaving?"

"I just need to be somewhere else...some place where there aren't any memories, aren't any ghosts haunting me day and night. I need a fresh start."

A bitter chuckle escaped my lips, and I blinked rapidly to hold back the onset of my sorrow. "You think running away will make it better? That you'll somehow find solace in a strange town?"

Jack's eyes came back up to meet mine, a sudden hardness

replacing the previous vulnerability. "No, I don't think running away will make everything better," he snapped, his voice echoing through the night. "Believe it or not, Sara, I'm not that naïve."

I flinched slightly at his biting remark, my shoulders sagging in resignation. I clutched tightly at the necklace hanging from my neck, a token of a happier time. "Don't go, Jack. Please." My plea floated about the space like a ghost itself, tethered to the tangible world by no more than a thread of hope.

He looked back at me, his expression heavy with uncertainty. "Can't you see, Sara? The longer I stay, the harder it is to breathe. Every corner of this town is soaked with the past, of those I've loved and lost."

A single tear escaped my eye, rolling down my cheek and disappearing into the fabric of my blouse. "This is about her, isn't it?" I asked, the realization cutting through me. Jack's decision wasn't about a fresh start—it was about the woman who had tossed him aside when things got tough. "This is about Ellie."

He didn't respond, which gave me my answer.

"Let her go, Jack. Clearly, she's moved on. Why can't you?"

"I wish it was that simple."

"Then make it simple. You have to let go. You can't keep living in the past. Why can't you put her behind you and see what you've got right here, standing in front of you?"

"I've tried, Sara. I really have, but every time I close my eyes, it's her face I see. Every night, I lie in bed and reach out, hoping against hope that she'll be there."

His words were like a dagger. I clutched the necklace tighter as the world around us shrank, pulled taut by the tension in the air. Silence fell like the suffocating weight of a shroud, pressing into every crevice. My breath hitched as Jack turned to me, his eyes seeming to glow with inner fire.

"How can I make you understand?" He took my hands, the heat from his touch searing into my skin. "This isn't just about her. It's about me, too. I'm the one who can't let go. Not yet."

"I can't stand here and watch you hurt yourself over this, Jack," I told him, pulling my hands free of his grip. My voice trembled, matching the quake in my heart. "Ellie made her choice. She ended things. And each day that you spend pining for her is a day you're choosing to lose yourself. So go, Jack. Chase after your ghost. But remember, she's just that—a ghost. And ghosts can't love you back."

* * *

The next day, Jack left Sims Chapel without so much as a goodbye. Time passed slowly after that. Days stretched into weeks, then months, and eventually years. As time went on, I wondered if I would ever find someone who would love me the way I wanted to be loved, the way I had wanted Jack to love me. I was angry at myself for wasting so many years pining for a man who clearly had no room for me in his heart. Years I could have spent finding someone who would truly value me and the love I had to offer.

For the next six years, I lived for myself. I traveled, met new people, and experienced things that opened my heart and mind in ways I hadn't expected. I never heard from Jack, and I didn't go looking for him either. As far as I was concerned, we were done. I had learned that you can't make someone stay, no matter how much you may want them to. Love, as I discovered, was a choice, and it was one Jack had decided not to make for me.

But that didn't mean I closed myself off to the idea of love. In fact, it was quite the opposite. Freed from the chains of my unrequited affection, it was during those years that I truly began to understand what love meant. Not the kind of love that clings and confines, but the sort that liberates and uplifts. I began to meet men who were not bound by ghosts of their past, men who could look at me and see me for who I was rather than a placeholder for a lost lover. I found a certain freedom in being seen, truly seen, in a way Jack never had. This was an awakening of sorts, like reaching the surface after being submerged for too long.

But for all the joy and excitement I experienced in those years, life wasn't without its trials and tribulations. Like the day my mother told me that she had been diagnosed with Huntington's chorea, a cruel disease that had claimed her own mother. I remember the hollow silence that followed her revelation, the numbness that spread through me as I struggled to process the devastating news. I also knew what this meant for me, that I was at risk of inheriting the same fate. But if my mother had taught me anything, it was to embrace life, to not shy away from its hardships but confront them head-on and grow stronger from the experience. She faced her diagnosis with grace and dignity, never allowing it to diminish her spirit or take away her zest for life. So I decided to do the same.

CHAPTER 16

Sims Chapel, TN

March 1960

After a long winter, spring finally arrived in Sims Chapel, infusing the town and my soul with a sense of renewal. The first blooms of daffodils painted the fields in lively hues of yellow and white, while the gentle chatters of birds echoed through the air.

One sunny afternoon, as I was tending to my small garden, I spotted a familiar figure walking up the driveway. I had to squint against the blinding sunlight, but there was no mistaking it. It was Jack.

He stood at a distance, his posture stiff and awkward, as if unsure whether he was welcome. As I approached, he ran his hands through his hair and then let them drop to his sides. He looked older somehow, more worn.

"Jack," I breathed out, the name bringing forth memories I had long buried. "Is it really you?"

His gaze met mine and for a moment, time seemed to stand still. "It's good to see you, Sara. I was worried you might have moved on."

I shook my head. "Me? Never. I'm right here where I've always been." The words slipped out before I could stop them, more sincere than I intended them to be.

He gave me a crooked smile and looked me over from head to toe. "You look great. How have you been?"

"Okay," I said. "And you?"

He looked away, as though gathering his thoughts. "I'm... better. It took me a while to figure things out, but I've made peace with it all now."

I took a few tentative steps forward, stopping just a few feet away from him. "Where did you go?"

"I've been all over," he replied, his gaze lost in the distant mountains. "I've seen the sun rise over the Grand Canyon, felt the salt spray on the Oregon coast. But none of it felt like home."

Home. The word lingered in the air.

"And what does feel like home?"

Jack turned to me, his lips drawn tight. "This. You." His voice was soft, almost a whisper, but it burned inside me like a wildfire. But I was determined not to fall for his charm again. I'd been burned too many times, and I couldn't afford the risk. "So, what brings you by?" I asked as I brushed past him and into the house.

"I was hoping we could talk. I have a lot of things I need to say to you."

I turned to face him, leaning against the kitchen counter. "Fine," I said, crossing my arms over my chest. "Talk."

For a moment, Jack just stood there, perhaps unsure of what to say. "I'm sorry, Sara," he said finally, his voice heavy with emotion. "For everything. For leaving you like I did, for not letting you in, for pushing you away when all you ever did was try to help me. I was so lost in my own pain that I failed to see the one person who still believed in me."

I swallowed hard, my mouth suddenly dry. I had to remind

myself that this was Jack, the same man who had left me heartbroken and alone. "Six years is a long time, Jack. You could have called...or written. You could have given me something to hold onto."

"I know," he replied, his face a picture of regret. "One of the many mistakes I've made that I wish I could take back." He shifted his gaze to the open window, where the late afternoon sun was slowly sinking behind the distant hills. "I've started writing again," he said, changing the subject. "My doctor suggested it, said it might help me process...everything. And it has, to an extent. Putting words to emotions I didn't even know I was feeling has helped me make sense of the chaos in my mind. I'm thinking of trying my hand at a novel soon."

I blinked at him, not sure what to make of this revelation. "That's good, Jack. You always enjoyed putting pen to paper."

He nodded, a sad smile playing on his lips. "I know I don't have the right to ask you for another chance, but I'm going to anyway. Your friendship means more to me than you know, and if there was any way I could go back in time and take it all back, I would."

I felt a pull in my chest, a yearning for the past. But I knew the past was just that, the past. "Jack, I appreciate you being honest with me, but it's not that simple. You can't just walk back into my life after five years and expect me to forget everything that happened. You say you've changed, well, so have I. I'm not about to get dragged back into the whirlwind I've spent half a decade escaping."

His eyes glossed over with resignation.

"Look, I'm glad you're home and that you're better. But I would prefer if we kept our distance. I've built a career for myself here, Jack. I've grown, both personally and professionally. I can't let that crumble on the whim of a man who couldn't value my affection when he had it." My voice was steady now, the words flowing out with an ease that surprised even me. "Besides that, my mother is ill, and I can't afford to let myself get tangled in emotional turmoil again. I need to be strong for her."

"I understand. And I'm genuinely sorry...about your mother...about everything." He backed toward the door. "It was nice seeing you again, Sara. I wish you all the happiness you deserve."

When he was gone, I sat down on the porch steps, letting the cool breeze touch my face. I took a deep breath, inhaling the scent of the rain from the earlier storm, and I thought about what I said. For the first time in my life, I had stayed true to myself. No longer was I the timid girl, living in the shadow of Jack's charisma. I was a woman now, who had found strength and resilience in her own solitude. I had weathered the storm of heartbreak and come out stronger on the other side.

CHAPTER 17

Present

"What made you stay after Jack left? Why not pack your things and leave, start a new life somewhere?"

I looked at Diane, then out toward the beach that I had come to love so much. "Sims Chapel was my home. My roots were there, my memories. Not to mention, my mother. I couldn't leave behind what was a core part of me. Besides, when Jack left, I was convinced he was gone for good. So I saw no need to run."

Diane nodded, her expression thoughtful. "And out of all the men you dated, there was never one who made you want to settle down?"

I laughed a little at the question. "Oh, there were a couple, but they weren't Jack. And perhaps that was the problem. I realized that I was comparing everyone to a man who didn't deserve to be the standard. Jack was a mirage, an illusion of love that had evaporated with time and distance. As much as it pained me to admit, I was holding on to the ghost of a man who had broken my heart, not once, but twice. A man who was supposed to be the love of my life but acted more like an anchor, dragging me to the depths of despair."

I studied my hands, gnarled with age, and thought about how much they had seen, how much they had done. These hands had planted seeds and harvested crops, cooked meals and mended clothes, rendered decisions that impacted lives and changed destinies. They had wiped away tears of despair and joy alike. They were the physical testament of my life—a life that was so much more than just Jack.

* * *

We broke for lunch and moved outside to the porch, where the ocean breeze tickled our faces, and the sun warmed our bones. The smell of the ocean mingled with the scent of Judy's homemade tomato soup and grilled cheese sandwiches.

"So, did you ever forgive him?"

"Who, Jack? Of course I did. As much as I wanted to hate him and curse his name every waking moment of my life, I knew that wouldn't bring me peace. Jack had made his choices, and I had to make mine. And I chose to forgive him, not because he deserved it, but because I did. I deserved to live a life free of bitterness and resentment."

Diane swallowed a bite of her sandwich before asking, "But you never pursued him again, did you?"

A faint smile made its way on to my lips as I recalled the weeks and months after Jack returned. "No," I said as the memories swirled around me. "But that didn't stop him from pursuing me."

Sims Chapel, TN

November 1961

"You look like you could use some company," I said to Jack, finding him sitting at the end of the dock.

Jack didn't turn around, but his shoulders dropped slightly as if in defeat. "Actually, I was enjoying the solitude."

I hesitated for a moment, then made my way toward him. "Do you want me to leave you alone?"

"No. I didn't mean it like that."

I settled down beside him, our shoulders brushing slightly. We sat quietly for a while as the waves lapped against the dock.

"My book is going to be published," he told me. "My agent called this afternoon to give me the news."

"That's fantastic, Jack," I said, my excitement tempered by his solemn expression. "So why the long face? Shouldn't you be out celebrating?"

"Probably..."

"But?"

"The whole time I was writing, I kept holding onto this hope that someday Ellie would come to her senses and return to me. Reliving all those memories almost made it real again, like she was still here. But now that I'm finished, I'm forced to face the reality that she's never coming back."

I wanted to tell him that he wasn't alone, that I'd stood where he currently did, teetering on the precipice of despair and loneliness. But I knew he had to find his own way through the darkness, just like I had.

"Speaking of news, I have some of my own," I said as I leaned back on my palms and changed the subject. "I'm thinking of taking a job in Asheville. I spoke to a friend of mine from college who called recently, and she said they're looking for a mathematics professor at Brevard College."

Jack's face was unreadable as he processed the information. "Asheville? But that's so far away."

"I know. But I feel like I need a change. A fresh start, you know?"

"Who will take care of your mother if you leave?"

"She's going to move in with her sister in Rogersville. She's been wanting to do that for a while anyway. Aunt Pete needs the company, and I think it will be good for them to be together."

"Can I ask why?"

"Do you really need me to spell it out for you?"

His brow furrowed as though he were trying to decipher a complex riddle. "Is this because of me?"

"No," I reassured him. "Not entirely. It's also because of her, and because of me. I'm tired of being the one who stays behind, waiting for life to happen. I want to go out there, make something of myself."

Jack flinched, as if I'd slapped him. His expression turned serious, his gaze dropping to the wooden planks beneath our feet. "What if I said I don't want you to go?"

I shrugged, giving him a sad smile. "That's the thing, Jack. This isn't about what you want. It's about what I want now."

As he stared out at the water, I could see his mind churning, wrestling with what I'd just said. He looked so small sitting there, his single silhouette against the backdrop of the lake and star-filled sky.

He finally turned to face me, a look of resignation in his eyes. "You're right," he whispered. "You have to do what's best for you. But know this, Sara. You've always been the most important person in my life. You always will be. And if there was anything I could say or do to make you change your mind, I'd do it in a heartbeat."

His sincerity made my heart ache. Deep down, I knew there was a part of me that would always be Jack's. We'd been through too much for me to simply erase him from my life. But there were things in life that required sacrifice, and sometimes, love was one of them.

"I know you would," I whispered back, my voice faltering a bit. "And if you'd asked me a few months ago, maybe I would have stayed. But things are different now. I'm different. It's funny, all I ever wanted was for you to look my way, to realize that what we could have together is better than anything you've lost. But you never did. At least, not entirely. And now, it's too late."

Jack looked at me, his eyes reflecting the pain I had just confessed. All around us, the night was still. Even the crickets had fallen silent. Without saying a word, Jack stood up and swept me into his arms. He carried me into the shack, closed the door behind us, and laid me down on the couch.

"Sara," he said, a strange mixture of vulnerability and determination in his voice. "I've been a fool. I've been so caught up in the past that I failed to see you." He gently traced the contour of my face with his thumb, his gaze softening as he met my eyes.

I was no fool. I knew where this was going. A part of me wanted to stop him, to tell him to say no more. Yet, another part of me felt like I was owed this for all the years of quiet longing, all the times I had been overlooked. This was my closure. I nodded, silently urging him to continue.

His hand moved from the curve of my face to entangle in my hair. He pulled me closer, our faces mere inches apart. "I love you, Sara," he whispered, making every cell in my body burn with desire.

"I love you, Jack."

"Stay with me tonight," he uttered, his voice thick with emotion, eyes pleading. I knew that this would eventually end in heartbreak, but in that moment, I didn't care. He wanted me, and I wanted him, and I was willing to sacrifice tomorrow for the sake of tonight. I nodded, surrendering myself into his arms.

His arms tightened around me, pulling me even closer, as if he were trying to weave us into a single entity.

I tilted my head back, allowing my forehead to rest against his own. Our breaths mingled, our hearts synced. For a moment, we simply existed together, savoring the heat and oneness that pulsed between us.

Finally, Jack reached for the buttons of my blouse, his fingers working them loose one by one. The fabric parted, revealing my soft skin to the cool night air. He traced his fingertips along the bare skin of my collarbone, setting my senses ablaze. His touch was both cautious and filled with longing, a fascinating contradiction that had me trembling in his arms.

He placed a soft kiss on my exposed shoulder, moving slowly upwards to my neck, leaving a trail of warmth. His hands moved lower, his fingers tracing the curve of my waist while he continued to nuzzle my neck, the touch of his lips feather-light against my skin.

I closed my eyes and surrendered myself to the blissful torment of his touch. I ran my fingers through his hair, tugging him closer, deepening the kiss. My heart pounded in my chest, echoing in my ears like a wild drumbeat.

As Jack's hands moved over me with a reverent touch, the last vestiges of my resistance crumbled. I clung to him, drowning in the sweet agony of his touch as it set my blood on fire. It felt as if we were existing in a private universe of our own creation—a world where the past no longer mattered, and the future was a horizon we could mold in our own image.

The room filled with an intoxicating mixture of emotions; our love that was no longer restrained, whispered confessions unearthed after years of secrets and the soft rustle of clothing being discarded. Each piece of fabric shed was like another chain from our past breaking free.

"Jack," I whispered against his lips, my breath hitching when his hands traced along my spine. A tremor went through my body, and I buried my face into his neck.

He paused for a moment and pulled back, his eyes dark pools that pierced my soul. "Sara," he whispered. The tenderness in his voice brought tears to my eyes. He had spoken my name countless times before, but never with such depth of emotion that now resonated in his voice. It was as if, in saying my name, he was accepting my love, our love, after years of denying it.

"I'm here," I replied softly, cupping his face with trembling hands, a fragile smile tugging my lips. "I've always been here."

My admission seemed to spark something within him, and Jack's eyes shone with an indescribable tenderness. He drew me closer until we were pressed together from head to toe. Heat radiated from him in waves, warming me in places I'd forgotten could feel warmth. With a deliberate slowness born of both reverence and desperation, he explored every inch of my body, leaving no part untouched.

Together, we crossed the line between friendship and lovers, a seismic shift, yet seamless in its unfolding. As our bodies entwined and moved against each other, I felt an overwhelming sense of belonging.

Each gasp echoed through the small space as we continued our fervent exploration. Our world contracted until nothing existed outside this room.

Our bodies danced to an unspoken rhythm, guided

by the magnetic pull of our hearts. Heat spread through me like wildfire as Jack's touch ignited a flame I didn't know was dormant. Every whisper, every caress, every gasp was etched into my heart, anchoring me in this moment of shared intimacy.

Time seemed to lose all meaning as we reveled in each other's embrace. Jack's fingers traced invisible patterns on my skin, sending shivers down my spine. As we kissed, I tasted the sweetness of newfound love and the bitterness of long-denied desire. I clung to him tighter, my nails digging into his broad shoulders, willing this moment to last forever.

The small shack creaked under the weight of our passion as if acknowledging the shift in our relationship. The fire that had been long smoldering between us had finally been set ablaze, radiating an unbearable heat that left us both yearning for more.

When it was over, we lay entwined, bodies still humming from the love they had shared. Jack traced the angles of my face with a gentleness that was almost reverential, his action echoing the soft glow of the hearth that painted our bodies in a warm, orange light.

I nestled closer against his chest, the steady beat of his heart lulling me into a sense of security. He played with strands of my hair, twirling them around absentmindedly. Our breaths synced, whispering stories to the silent night outside.

* * *

After our night of passion, we drove back to my place under the cover of darkness and fell into a deep, well-deserved slumber. The next morning, I woke in Jack's arms. The moment I had waited for had finally come, and it was utterly perfect. Jack was still in a deep sleep, his chest rising and falling with each breath.

His face was buried in my hair, strands of it tangled between his fingers. His firm grip around my waist was comforting, making me feel cherished and loved.

I cautiously extricated myself from his arms without waking him and slid out of the bed, my feet touching the cold wooden floor. The room was filled with the pale glow of dawn, casting soft shadows across the antique furniture. I walked toward the window, my bare feet padding silently across the floor.

Drawing back the curtains, I saw snow falling softly outside. The world was a white canvas, velvety flakes dancing in the muted morning light. The sight made my heart flutter in childish delight. I went to my closet and chose my thickest red woolen sweater, pulling it over my nightdress as I tiptoed into the hallway. Assuming Jack would sleep a while longer, I made a pot of coffee and prepared breakfast for one.

As I sat at the kitchen table, sipping my coffee and nibbling on buttered toast, the quiet of the house wrapped itself around me like a blanket. I stared out of the frosted window at the mesmerizing dance of the snowflakes, their descent hypnotic. The world felt distant and hushed, as if time itself was observing a moment of silence.

Suddenly, I felt a pair of strong arms encircle me from behind. A warm body pressed against my back, and the scent of Jack's aftershave wafted into my nostrils. I smiled to myself as he buried his face in the crook of my neck, his scruffy beard tickling my skin. Jack's voice was rough with sleep as he murmured his morning greeting into my ear.

"Good morning," he said, pressing a soft kiss to my neck. Without breaking the embrace, he reached for a piece of toast, his fingers delicately brushing mine as he did. He took a bite, crumbs falling onto the table before he rested his chin on my shoulder.

"Oh," he said, noticing the morning's unexpected snowfall. "I didn't think it would snow."

"Neither did I. It's beautiful, isn't it?"

He hummed in agreement, his breath tickling my ear. "Almost as beautiful as you."

I responded with a light laugh, a blush creeping up on my cheeks.

Jack released me from his grasp and moved to the kitchen window, his gaze drawn to the winter wonderland beyond. His silhouette against the soft light was captivating; the strong line of his jaw, the broad expanse of his shoulders, and the way his hand rested lightly on the frosted glass. He seemed to be lost in thought, a serene smile playing on his lips.

"We should make a snowman," he said with enthusiasm.

"What?"

"A snowman. We haven't done that in years. Remember the first one we made? We must have been seven or eight."

I laughed at the memory—one of those vivid, happy moments that had permanently etched itself onto my heart. Lewis had been barely five then, his eyes wide with excitement as he'd rolled the first snowball.

"Yes, I remember," I said, the corners of my mouth pulling into a reminiscent smile. "Okay, let's do it."

We spent the next hour laughing and playing in the snow, our breath misting in the frosty air. The snow was perfect for packing, and soon a round snowman began to take shape. Jack rolled the base, his broad shoulders straining under the effort, while I crafted the head.

As I worked, carefully smoothing the snow until it was

perfectly round, Jack smeared some on my face. Shocked, I turned to him, spluttering and laughing at his childish antics. In response, I scooped up a handful of snow and hurled it at him, hitting him squarely in the chest. His laugh filled the air, the sound echoing off the surrounding trees and adding to the magic of the moment.

When our hands were numb, we returned to the house and made love by the fire. As our bodies entwined and the glow of the flames flickered across our skin, the connection seemed to encompass our entire history. Each touch a memory, each breath a promise.

"Remember this moment," Jack whispered into my ear.

I turned toward him, my eyes meeting his in the soft light. "I will," I said, pressing myself closer to him. "For as long as I live."

CHAPTER 18

Present

"After all that time, you finally got what you wanted," said Diane, bringing me back to the present.

"Yes. I felt like I was floating, suspended in a moment of absolute clarity and joy...like every piece of me had found its place, its purpose."

We finished our soup and pushed the bowls to the center of the table.

"So, if you got what you wanted, what finally happened that made you leave Sims Chapel for good?"

I wanted to tell her it was a combination of things, that there wasn't just one moment, one reason. But the truth was far simpler, far more painful. "My past finally caught up with me," I said quietly, studying the last bite of grilled cheese on my plate. "That, and Ellie returned."

"Ellie? But I thought she was out of the picture."

"Oh, she was," I said, recalling the days when it was just me and Jack. "But then something terrible and unexpected happened, and just like that, she was back for good."

Sims Chapel, TN

May 1962

"She's dead." The words came as a whisper, almost too soft to hear. Jack shut the door behind him, his expression a grim mask of disbelief. "Clara's dead."

I froze as my heart dropped into my stomach, the weight of the news pulling me toward the floor. Clara...the woman who meant so much to Jack, who meant so much to us all, was gone.

"How?" I asked, my voice thin and far away.

Jack didn't meet my eyes. Instead, he moved past me, over to the window that overlooked the broad oak trees and the dusty road beyond. "Heart attack," he said, hardly able to choke out the words. "I thought she was sleeping... I tried everything I could to save her, but there was nothing I could do."

I stood there, my heart aching for the pain he was in, for the loss of Clara who was like a mother to us all, and for the oncoming storm I knew was about to hit.

* * *

The news of Clara's death spread like wildfire. The whole town seemed to sink into a quiet sorrow, but no one more than Jack. He kept himself busy with work, avoiding everyone, even me. He grew distant, lost in his thoughts and grief. I tried to draw him out, but he seemed locked in a fortress of his own making.

Time ticked by slowly, each minute an agonizing eternity. And somewhere amidst the sorrow, a terrible thought took root in my mind, one I dared not utter aloud—would Clara's death spark Ellie's return?

Then one morning, I received a phone call from Matthew

down at the dock letting me know that a woman was there, and that Jack had taken her for a ride in his boat. That's when I knew. Ellie was back.

* * *

When Jack got home from work that evening, I was in the middle of making supper.

"You're late," I said as he walked through the front door. I handed him a glass of sweet tea and kissed him on the lips.

Jack eased into his favorite chair. "Sorry. I stopped at the cemetery to talk to George."

"Everything okay?"

He tipped his head in a yes.

"Are you hungry?"

"Starving."

"Supper's almost ready. We're having your favorite—pot roast with potatoes and carrots." I checked on supper and returned a moment later. "So, a little birdie told me Ellie's back in town. You haven't seen her, have you?"

Jack looked up and eyed me suspiciously. "No, but you knew she'd come...for the funeral."

"Nevertheless, I imagine it's only a matter of time before she comes looking for you."

Jack narrowed his brows at me. "What makes you say that?"

"I may be a lot of things, Jack, but naïve isn't one of them. I remember how crazy she was about you."

Jack upended his tea glass before responding with an edge in his voice. "That was a long time ago, Sara."

"Regardless, you know what they say about old flames."

"Are we really going to have this conversation again? Like I've told you countless times, Ellie and I are ancient history.

Whatever fire may have existed burned out long ago."

"Let's hope you're right." I shot him a look of warning. "For your sake, and for hers."

The following morning, I slept in while Jack went down into the kitchen to make breakfast. When I finally joined him, he was halfway through his plate of food.

"I was thinking," he said as he chewed, "maybe after the funeral, we could get out of here and spend a few days in the mountains."

"The mountains? What brought this on?"

He shrugged. "We've both been busy lately, me at the dock and you with your mother. I just thought we could use some time away, that's all."

"And you promise this has nothing to do with Ellie?"

"Promise."

"In that case..." I went over and sat on his lap, straddling him and wrapping my arms around his neck. "Some time away would be nice." After kissing him passionately, I stood up and began to clear the breakfast dishes.

"Good," he said, seeming a bit preoccupied. "I'll make the arrangements."

Despite Jack's reassurances, a nagging worry lodged itself in the back of my mind. I couldn't shake the feeling that Ellie's return had stirred up old emotions, ones that could disrupt our peaceful life together.

To confirm my suspicions, I decided to pay Ellie a visit. I'd heard from a friend that she was staying at Clara's, so I drove over there that very same day. Armed with a steely resolve and the knowledge that Jack had lied about seeing her, I took a deep breath and knocked on Clara's door.

"Sara," said Ellie as she swung the door wide, her eyebrows

rising a notch. "I almost didn't recognize you. Golly, what a nice surprise. Please come in."

"Are you sure? I don't want to impose."

Ellie gave a dismissive wave. "You're no imposition, and it's nice to see a familiar face." She showed me inside. "My mother and sister won't be back for a while, so we have the place to ourselves."

"I can't remember the last time I was in this house." My eyes wandered around the room. "I'm terribly sorry for your loss. Miss Clara was a wonderful woman."

"Thank you. That's sweet of you to say. I was just about to sit down to lunch. Care to join me?"

"Yes, thank you."

Ellie offered me a seat in the living room, then brought out a plate of sandwiches and two glasses of tea. "I didn't realize you still lived around here," she said as she relaxed into the chair. "What brings you out this way?"

I set my glass on the table and took a moment to gather my thoughts. "To offer my condolences...and to speak with you about Jack."

"Jack? What about him?"

I stiffened under Ellie's gaze, a mask of determination forming on my face. "I know you went to see him yesterday."

"Yes. I went by the dock to see the changes he'd made. It's a first-class operation now."

I nervously sipped my tea before responding. "Did he happen to tell you that he and I are together?"

If my revelation bothered her, her face didn't show it. "No, he didn't."

"Figures."

"How long?" Ellie asked.

"Long enough."

Ellie managed a weak smile. "Well, I'm happy for you, Sara. You're a good person. I've always thought so."

"Thank you." The muscles in my face relaxed, making room for a smile of my own. "And don't worry, someday you'll find that special someone, too. I just know it."

When we had finished eating, Ellie walked me to the door. "Will I see you at the funeral tomorrow?"

"Of course. Jack and I wouldn't miss it."

Now that Ellie knew about Jack and me, a weight had been lifted from my shoulders. The looming uncertainty and the fear of how she might react was gone. Now, I could only hope that she would accept our relationship and let us be.

* * *

The funeral was a somber affair. The gray clouds above mirrored the mood of the mourners, all clad in black and speaking in hushed voices. Rain fell from the sky in sheets, soaking the earth and turning it into a muddy mess. Ellie was there, of course, along with her mother and sister. Their faces were pale and drawn, eyes red-rimmed. From a distance, I observed Ellie's every move. She glanced at Jack every now and then, her gaze lingering just a second too long. It was as if a silent conversation was taking place between them, one that I couldn't hear or understand. A sharp pang of jealousy jabbed at my heart, making me wince inwardly.

After the funeral, Jack went to Clara's house to prepare dinner for the mourners, while I went to see my mother. I knew it was risky leaving Jack and Ellie alone, but I also knew that I couldn't let my insecurities dictate my actions. My mother, who had fallen ill, needed me too.

During the drive over, I contemplated my decision to thwart Jack's proposal all those years ago. As time went on, I had convinced myself that it was the right choice. The only choice. But as I navigated the narrow roads leading to my mother's house, I wondered if I had made a terrible mistake. If he had proposed, Ellie might have turned him down. Or perhaps they would have married, only to find that they weren't right for each other. Maybe then he would have come back to me.

All of the 'what-ifs' were gradually eating away at my sanity. I parked in front of my mother's house, the familiar sight of the crimson roses she loved so much doing little to soothe my troubled mind and went inside.

"So, how are things going with Jack?" she asked after dinner.

I hesitated a moment before responding, picking at the remnants of my meal. "Good," I said, hoping my voice would hide my concern.

"Just good?"

"It's complicated," I said, forcing a smile. Her eyes bored into me, seeming to search for the underlying issue.

"Is there something you're not telling me?"

I sighed, the weight of Ellie's return and my secret pressing against my chest, begging for release. "Ellie's back," I finally confessed, "to pay her final respects."

My mother's stoic expression faltered ever so slightly. "And?"

"And it feels like it did before, like I'm on the outside looking in."

"But that was so long ago, Sara. And they've been broken up for years. Besides, you're with Jack now, not her."

"I know. But I can't help but feel like the past is repeating itself. The way they look at each other... It's like I don't exist."

She reached across the table and took my hand, her fingers frail, but the grip firm. "Listen to me, Sara. The past is the past, and there's nothing any of us can do about that. But don't let fear and insecurity ruin what you have now. Besides, Jack is a good man, a loyal man, and he loves you."

I wanted to believe her, but the seeds of doubt had already been sown.

"Have you talked to him about it?" she asked as she cleared the table.

I nodded briefly, getting up to help her. "But I didn't press the issue."

"And why not?"

"I don't know. Fear, maybe. Or guilt." I turned on the water and washed the plates before setting them on the rack to dry.

"Guilt? What do you have to feel guilty about, sweetheart?"

After wiping my hands on the towel, I took a deep breath, collecting my thoughts. "Do you remember the summer that Ellie first came to visit? The summer I turned nineteen?"

"Yes, I remember."

I leaned against the counter, crossing my arms over my chest. "I spent most of that summer tutoring Ellie when I should have been on the lake with Jack."

"How could I forget? That's when you thought you'd lost Jack forever. And I also remember telling you to give it time, that things would work out for the best. And look, I was right."

"Something happened that summer that I never told you about, something that has stayed with me since."

"What is it, dear?"

I cleared my throat, my hands trembling slightly. Finally, I opened my mouth and told her everything—about the ring, about Jack's planned proposal, and about the phone call I'd made to Marie Spencer.

"You... You did *what*? Oh Sara..."

I gave a solemn nod, accepting the judgment I saw in her eyes. "That's why Marie showed up early and took Ellie home."

"And Jack?"

"He was devastated. He couldn't understand why Ellie left without a word. And I... I couldn't bring myself to tell him the truth."

Mother clucked her tongue sympathetically, absorbing the weight of my confession.

"As the summer ended," I continued, "I prepared to return to college, all the while feeling like I was running from my guilt. Jack and I drifted apart after that... We stayed friendly, but it was never the same."

"Oh, Sara." She sighed deeply, putting a hand to her heart. "That is quite a heavy secret to bear."

"I've carried it for years," I said, my voice thick with regret. "I thought in time the guilt would fade, but it hasn't."

"A love lost is a hard thing. But the past is the past. We can't change what has been done."

"I know. But sometimes, in the quiet of the night, I wonder if things could have been different, would have been different if I had just let them play out naturally."

"Perhaps they could have," she mused. "But we will never know for certain. What matters now is what you do moving forward."

For a moment, our thoughts were consumed by the revelation. The hum of summer insects outside served as a reminder of that fateful summer so many years ago.

"What do you plan on doing now?"

"I'm not sure yet. If I tell him, I risk undoing the relationship we've built. But if I don't, this will continue to eat at me."

Worry lines creased her forehead. "And you don't think Jack will figure it out on his own?"

I shook my head, thinking that if it hadn't happened by now, it would never happen. "I don't see how."

"For your sake, I hope you're right. Secrets have a way of coming to the surface eventually," she warned gently. "And it might be better if Jack hears it from you rather than someone else."

I looked into her wise, compassionate eyes as a lump formed in my throat. "I know... I've thought about that. But the fear of losing him for good always stops me."

"Sara, dear. If Jack truly cares for you as much as I think he does, he will understand. He may be hurt or angry at first, but if your bond is as strong as you believe it to be, he will come around. But," she continued, her expression turning serious, "if you choose to continue to keep this from him, and he finds out another way, you may lose him forever."

I sat quietly, contemplating my mother's words. I felt a rush of emotions—fear, relief and something akin to hope. Perhaps she was right, maybe it was time I faced the past and finally come clean. Either way, one thing was for certain—I was willing to do whatever it took to keep from losing Jack.

CHAPTER 19

When I woke the next morning, I was filled with a new resolve. As much as I wanted to be honest with Jack, I trusted that if I just gave it time, Ellie would be gone, and our lives could return to normal. So I decided to bury my secret even deeper, hoping it would never see the light of day.

After making sure Mother was comfortable, I set out for Dandridge, where I did a little shopping. I bought a new dress and some ribbons for my hair, along with a special outfit for my trip with Jack. I even picked up some steaks for dinner, hoping that we could celebrate Ellie's departure and a return to normalcy.

By the time I got to Jack's place, it was nearly dusk, the sky a breathtaking mix of purples and golds. I paused in the driveway, taking in the sight of our house, nestled among the trees. The sight gave me a flicker of hope that maybe life could indeed return to normal, that perhaps I had survived the storm a second time.

I parked my car alongside the white picket fence and retrieved my bags from the back seat. As I eased up the walkway, I could see Jack through the window, a drink in his hand. I felt a knot tighten in my stomach.

The front door creaked open before I even reached the porch step. Jack stood there, his face ashen and his eyes vacant.

"There you are," I said, surprised to find him home at this

hour. I set the groceries on the kitchen counter and kissed him. "I wasn't expecting you until later."

"Yeah, well, Matthew agreed to close up, so I decided to come home early."

I smiled, but he didn't smile back. "I'm glad you did because I stopped to see Gary and had him cut us a couple of steaks."

"What's the occasion?"

"There isn't one. I'm just happy things are finally returning to normal."

"And by that you mean—?"

I cut my eyes to him. "Back to the way things were before the funeral." I unpacked the bags and asked if he wanted to eat now or later.

He downed the rest of his drink, then got up and eased toward the living room. "I'm not really that hungry."

"What's the matter with you?"

"You've always been honest with me, right? I mean, you wouldn't lie to me, would you?"

I froze, my hands clenched in fists at my sides. "Heavens, no. What's got you all worked up?"

"There's something I need to ask you, something important, and I want you to be honest."

The world seemed to be closing in around me. I found an open chair and sat, my legs too weak to stand. "All right."

"Why didn't you tell me you called Marie Spencer to let her know I was planning to propose to Ellie?"

His words hit me all at once, like a gust of wind knocking the breath out of me. "W-What are you talking about?"

"All this time I thought her showing up unexpectedly was just a terrible coincidence, or bad luck, but I was wrong. It was you."

The room spun. My heart pounded in my chest like a wild trapped animal. "Who told you that? Was it Ellie?"

"What if it was? Do you deny it?"

"She's lying, Jack. Can't you see that? She's trying to do whatever she can to steal you from me again."

"Steal me. Really, Sara? Are you seriously going to sit there and tell me you didn't call Marie the night you saw the engagement ring? I saw the look on your face that night at the dock. You were angry, weren't you? And you thought if you could get Marie here before I had a chance to ask Ellie, you'd still have a shot, didn't you?"

I wilted under his gaze. I considered denying it again and spinning some tale of misunderstanding and confusion, but the look in his eyes was too knowing, too hurt. The truth was out.

"Why would you do that to me? I thought you loved me?"

"I do love you. Don't you see? That's why I did it. Ellie never loved you, not the way I do. All she ever did was break your heart."

"You're right. She did break my heart, but what you did was worse. You had no right."

"No right?" Fighting mad, I jumped to my feet. "I've been in love with you from the beginning, long before Ellie Spencer blew into town with her fancy clothes and uppity attitude. And who was there after she broke your heart, huh? Who has always been there, picking up the pieces, patiently waiting? Me, that's who. So don't tell me I didn't have a right." I stopped and took a breath, feeling as if I might cry. "But none of that matters now. Ellie's gone, hopefully for good this time, and you need to accept that." I turned on my heel and started toward the kitchen.

"Actually, she isn't."

I took a step, stopped, and turned back. Had I heard him

right? "What did you say?"

Jack shook his head. "Ellie isn't gone. In fact, she's staying."

Confusion reigned. "I-I don't understand. She was supposed to leave this morning."

"You're right, she was. But I asked her to stay, and she agreed."

"Absolutely not! I won't allow it."

"I'm afraid you have no say in the matter. And before you say another word..." He held up a hand. "Let me tell you how things are going to be from now on." He took a step toward me, his jaw clenched so tight, the muscles rippled through his skin. "You have one hour to pack your things and leave this house. After that, I don't care where you go or what you do, but you're not welcome here anymore. Is that clear?"

"Jack, you can't be serious. Please give me another chance. Are you willing to throw away what we have because of something that happened when we were teenagers?"

"Yes, I am," he said firmly. "And despite what you think, I loved you, Sara. We could have had a future together. But I won't be in a relationship built on lies." He grabbed his keys and headed for the door.

"Where are you going?"

"Out. One hour," he said, holding up a finger, "and you'd better be gone when I get back." Jack slammed the door behind him, leaving me weeping on the living room floor.

Present

When I finished telling Diane about that painful day, my eyes were blurred with tears. The memories, still so vivid, stung like salt on an open wound.

"I...I don't know what to say," Diane said, her voice full of sympathy. "I had no idea it ended like that."

"Yeah, well..." I wiped the tears from my cheeks with the back of my hand. "That night was the hardest night of my life. After my fight with Jack, I drove to my aunt's house and wept until the early morning hours. What was left of my heart was shattered, the remnants strewn about like shards of glass. Mother, who seemed to always have the answers, was at a loss for words. Instead, she stroked my hair, her comforting presence the only consolation to me."

"What happened next?"

"The next few days were a blur. I was a ghost, just going through the motions of life. I stumbled through breakfast, fumbling a pot of coffee that shattered on the kitchen floor. Tears sprung anew at the sight of the broken glass, an echo of my devastation. I didn't know how to pick up the pieces, no more than I knew how to mend my broken heart. Later, I sat on the porch, staring out at the woods. The trees swayed with a rhythm that mocked me. Each gust of wind like a taunt, a reminder of the world moving on while I was trapped in my own private torment. A piece of me wished Jack would change his mind, that he would find it in his heart to forgive me and give me a chance to make things right. But I knew it was a fool's hope. Jack had made his stance crystal clear. My past transgressions were unforgivable in his eyes, and there was nothing I could say or do that would change that. It would be years later before I realized that the seeds of my destiny were sown that warm May evening."

"Was that the moment everything changed for you?"

"Yes. I didn't know it at the time, but looking back, I see

it clearly now. That was the pivot, the hinge on which my life swung in a new direction."

Diane asked if I needed a break, but I shook my head, knowing that if I didn't do this now, while my emotions were raw, I would never get through it. "No," I told her, summoning every ounce of strength I had. "I need to finish this. I need to get this all out."

PART 2

CHAPTER 20

Kitty Hawk, NC

May 1962

With my life in pieces and nowhere to turn, I drove east until I ran out of road. The choice to leave Sims Chapel, especially with my mother in poor health, was a difficult one, but I knew it was necessary. Otherwise, I would have drowned in a sea of my own despair.

As the sun broke the horizon, setting ablaze a thinning fog, I found myself at the edge of a forgotten coastal town, its name barely legible on the crooked wooden sign that swayed gently in the salty sea breeze. I parked the car and sat on the hood, taking a few minutes to clear my head. Before me lay a vast expanse of ocean, its deep blue depths as turbulent as the emotions within me.

As waves crashed against the shore, my thoughts drifted toward happier times. The laughter-filled afternoons, the warm summer nights, and the tender promises of forever echoed through my mind. But now they were nothing but distant memories.

The early morning fog took its time to roll away, allowing me a moment of solitude before the town began to stir. Standing at the edge of the world, I felt insignificant and lost, my troubles swallowed up by the ocean before me.

A lighthouse stood tall and solitary in the distance, reminding me of my own isolation, my own need for guidance. I ripped a page from the notebook I'd brought with me and began to write, my thoughts spilling onto the paper as freely as the waves on the shore. I wrote of love and loss, of dreams dashed and hopes unfulfilled. My pen moved in time with my heartbeat, the words evidence of my despair. Amidst my melancholy prose, I penned lines of resilience, whispers of strength I didn't know I possessed. When I was finished, I closed my eyes and let the breeze catch the paper, carrying it out over the ocean. The letter was only a speck against the seascape, but it was my speck, a part of me set free to be embraced by the unending azure. As it drifted out of view, an inexplicable lightness came over me, a small burden lifted off my heavy heart.

Tired and hungry, I turned back, leaving traces of my sorrow behind. The town was beginning to wake. Lights were coming on in the beachside row houses while the smell of biscuits and bacon wafted from the restaurant on the pier. My stomach grumbled at the familiar scent.

The restaurant was a small, cozy building in the center of the pier. It had a thatched roof and a welcome sign above the door that read, "Hawks Haven." Stepping inside, I was immediately enveloped in warmth and the comforting smell of coffee brewing somewhere in the back. The place was already bustling with life. Early risers sat at the counter nursing cups of coffee and reading newspapers, while others were gathered at tables, devouring plates of pancakes and eggs. Behind the counter, a young woman hurried about, her face lighting up as soon as she spotted me.

"Morning!" she called, her voice as warm as the aroma

wafting from the kitchen. "Have a seat anywhere you like, and I'll be with you in a minute."

I chose a booth by the window where I could still see the expanse of the ocean. It was exactly as I had imagined it, the view dotted by distant sailing ships, their white sails billowing in the wind.

The woman, her name tag cheerfully announcing her as "Judy," came over, a worn-out notebook in hand, to take my order. She was tall, with a shock of red hair and freckles that dotted her cheeks like fallen stars. Her eyes were a striking shade of blue, similar to the color of the ocean just outside the window, and she had an easy-going charm about her that was instantly likable. "What'll it be this morning?" she asked as she smacked her gum. "We've got biscuits and gravy, or perhaps some scrambled eggs and bacon?"

"I'll have the scrambled eggs, please. And a cup of black coffee."

She nodded and hurried off toward the kitchen. Left alone, I turned my attention back out to the ocean. The last twenty-four hours had been a whirlwind of emotions, and I felt as though I had been carried adrift by the ferocious storm that was my life. Watching the steady ebb and flow of the waves calmed my spirit and, for a moment, I forgot about the chaos of yesterday.

Judy returned promptly with a steaming cup of coffee and placed it in front of me. "Your breakfast will be up shortly," she said, before moving off to attend to another patron.

I wrapped my hands around the warm cup, drawing comfort from its heat. I took a sip and savored the bitter, rich taste as it slipped down my throat. The coffee seeped its warmth into me, thawing the chill that had settled in my bones.

Outside, the sun climbed higher in the sky, spreading

a warm glow over the slate-gray of the ocean. The seagulls were wheeling about now, squawking and nosediving into the water, their white bodies stark against the blue of the sky. The previously distant sailing ships seemed to have drawn closer, their sails catching the sunlight and making them look like ghostly apparitions on the horizon.

A plate clattered onto the table, breaking me out of my reverie. "There you go," Judy announced, setting down a heaping plate filled with scrambled eggs and crispy bacon strips. There was also a side of toast smeared with butter, all golden and glistening under the soft morning light filtering through the window. The aroma of the food was comforting, homely. My stomach grumbled in anticipation.

"Thank you," I said, offering her a grateful smile.

"You're welcome. Say, you're not from around here, are you?"

I shook my head, feeling the heat touch my cheeks. "How can you tell?"

"It's not hard to spot a stranger in this town." Judy tilted her head to the side. "Let me guess... Georgia? Tennessee?"

"East Tennessee."

"I thought I recognized that accent. I was born in Chattanooga myself."

"That's only a couple of hours from my hometown. So, how'd you end up here?"

"Long story. Let's just say that life has a way of steering you in places you never expected."

"Isn't that the truth," I replied, thinking of my own situation. "I'm Sara, by the way."

"It's nice to meet you, Sara. My name's Judy."

We fell into an easy conversation after that, discussing our shared southern roots and love of small-town life. As it turned out, Judy was on her own, having lost her mother a couple of years earlier to cancer. She'd been left this restaurant and had chosen to keep it running as a way to honor her mother.

"What brings you to Kitty Hawk, Sara?"

The smile ran away from my face. I wasn't ready to tell anyone the real reason, least of all a complete stranger. "Just needed a fresh start," I said, hoping that my vague answer would suffice.

She gave me a long, thoughtful look but didn't push any further. "In that case, let me be the first to welcome you here. Are you planning on staying or are you just passing through?"

"I don't know. I think I might stay. I like the quietness here," I said, my gaze drifting toward the window again. The ships were now mere specks, washed away in the brightening morning light. "But I'll need to find a job and a place to stay. You don't know who I might talk to about those things, do you?"

"That depends." Judy leaned forward, resting her elbows on the table and interlacing her fingers. "What kind of work are you looking for?"

"I was a teacher back home... High school math. So, something in education would be ideal."

"So you're educated?"

I nodded in response.

"I'm afraid I don't know anything about teaching jobs. You'd have to talk to someone at the school board about that. But if you're interested in working here, I might be able to help. How are your waitressing skills?"

"I've never worked in a restaurant before, if that's what you're asking. But I've poured more cups of coffee and sweet tea than I can count...and I've taken orders, too...lots of them.

Besides that, I'm a hard worker, and I learn quickly."

She seemed to be pondering this, her brows furrowing slightly as she looked me over. "To be honest, I was hoping for someone with a bit more experience, but I guess beggars can't be choosers, can they? The truth is, I'm in a bit of a pickle. I happen to be one waitress short right now, and it's all Rosie and I can do to keep up. That's her, over there." She pointed to a young woman about our age—early thirties—with dark hair pulled back tightly into a bun, balancing a full tray of breakfast plates. "So, if you want it, the job's yours."

"You mean it?"

Judy tipped her head in a nod. "Once the breakfast rush dies down, I'll have Rosie show you around."

"Thank you," I said, hardly believing my luck. "Now, I just need to find a place to stay."

Judy's eyebrows rose slightly, as though she had been expecting this. "This is your lucky day. I have a room upstairs that just happens to be vacant. It's not much, but the rent is cheap, and it would give you a place to stay until you find something more permanent."

I wanted to hug her right then and there, but I figured that might be pushing it. So instead, I extended my hand across the table. "I'll take it."

"Wonderful. Welcome aboard." Judy stood and dusted the crumbs from her apron. "Tell you what, why don't I let you finish your breakfast in peace, then we can discuss next steps."

I was so excited I could hardly eat, but I managed to finish my meal, my mind spinning with the sudden turn of events. As I sipped the last of my coffee, I looked around the bustling restaurant. The clattering of dishes, the hum of conversation, the occasional burst of laughter that cut through it all. This was more than just a place to eat. It was a haven, a community hub.

When the crowd thinned, Rosie came over and introduced herself.

"So, Judy says you're our new waitress. I'm Rosalie, but everybody calls me Rosie. You can too, if you like." Rosie was every bit as friendly as Judy and had a smile that seemed to light up the whole restaurant. And her accent was unlike anything I'd ever heard—a Southern drawl with a hint of Spanish, like she'd spent years in two vastly different places.

"Hi, Rosie. I'm Sara."

With pleasantries out of the way, Rosie led me around the restaurant, pointing out where things were situated and explaining the routines. As we walked, she described the regular customers and their peculiar habits, which ranged from the old fisherman who took his coffee black with a dash of salt, to the eccentric painter who always ordered blueberry pie. There was a rhythm to this place, a certain harmony that resonated with the ebb and flow of the ocean.

Once I had familiarized myself with the restaurant, Rosie brought me back to Judy, who led me upstairs to the small room I would be renting. The space was cozy with a single bed, a wooden dresser, and a window that looked out onto the beach. The room smelled strongly of sea salt and old wood, which I found oddly comforting.

"This has been vacant for a while," said Judy, leaning against the doorframe. "It'll need a good cleaning, but it's got a certain charm, don't you think?"

I nodded, stepping toward the window and taking in the view. The ocean stretched on for miles with waves lazily lapping against the shore. The beach was almost deserted, save for a lone figure walking a dog along the water's edge. It was peaceful, serene. "It's perfect."

Judy grinned, pushing herself off the doorframe. "You've got your own private bathroom through there," she said, pointing to a small door on the left. "And if you ever need anything, my room is just down the hall."

"Wait, so you live here, too?"

Judy laughed. "Of course. This isn't just my restaurant. It's also my home, which is why I take pride in making sure everyone who passes through feels comfortable and welcome. But don't worry, I know how to keep to myself. You'll have plenty of peace and quiet."

The notion of sharing a home with my employer was new to me, but not entirely disagreeable. The way Judy spoke made it feel less like a business arrangement and more like being welcomed into an extended family. I had been looking for a fresh start, and the promise of becoming part of this unique, seaside community was unexpectedly appealing.

"What about Rosie? Does she live here, too?"

"No. She's got her own place, just across the street."

"I see. She's not from around here, is she?"

Judy chuckled. "No. She was born in Texas, but her family is originally from Mexico. They moved to Corpus Christi before she was born. She's got quite the story, Rosie does, but I'll let her tell it. Well, I should get back downstairs and give you time to get settled."

"Thank you, Judy. You have no idea how much all of this means to me."

Her eyes crinkled at the corners. "You're more than welcome. We're happy to have you here. The dinner rush starts around six. You're welcome to join us downstairs if you're up for it. Oh, and if you're wondering about things to do, I'm afraid there isn't much. But there's a bar a few blocks up that has a good band. And there's a movie theater that Rosie and I frequent on Roanoke Island, which is about a half hour from here. You're more than welcome to tag along."

"Thanks. I'll keep that in mind."

Judy gave me a final friendly nod before she walked away, leaving me to adjust to my new surroundings. The room was simple but homey. I went to my car and grabbed some of my belongings, then unpacked my suitcase, placing my clothes in the wooden dresser and setting a few personal items–a photograph of my mother, a well-worn novel, and a small potted plant—on the bedside table. The ocean breeze ruffled the curtains as I opened the window to let in the fresh air, and I took a deep breath. It smelled like home, not like Sims Chapel, but like a place where I belonged.

Falling back on the bed, I closed my eyes, letting the sound of the waves wash over me. Despite the odds, I had done it. I had survived the tumultuous journey that brought me here, and I was determined to make the most of this new beginning.

Present

With a long exhale, I called it a day. Despite my exhaustion, I had made it through the most difficult part of my journey. Now, all I wanted to do was rest.

Judy prepared a simple dinner of fish and chips, and Diane and I indulged in the hearty meal. Afterward, we retreated to the back lawn and started a fire, sitting in Adirondack chairs and sipping wine. Our conversation flowed easily, filled with stories and laughter, the warmth of companionship as welcoming as the crackling fire.

"Tell me," Diane said, "about that departure. Why Kitty Hawk? Why not Wilmington or Edenton?"

The truth was, I didn't have an answer that would make any sense. I had no family here, no old friends waiting for me. "Impulse," I said, reflecting on the decisions I'd made during that drive, taking a right instead of a left, turning here when the road went there. "Nothing more."

Diane was quiet a moment, staring up into the night sky. "It's funny, isn't it, how something as simple as going one direction instead of another can have such a profound impact on the course of our lives."

"Yes, it is. But sometimes, that's all we can do—choose a path and see where it leads us."

As the night wore on and the alcohol did its job, Diane opened up more about her life in Charlotte.

"I was raised there," she said as she stared into her wine glass. "But I wasn't born there. At least, I don't think I was. I was adopted, so I can't be entirely certain."

"Adopted? What was that experience like?"

"My parents, or rather, my adoptive parents, were wonderful people who provided me with every comfort that life could offer. A nice home, good education, and all the love a child could need. But there was always this void, this missing piece. When I asked about my birth parents, they would always avoid the topic, as if it was a deeply buried secret that could never see the light. I would inquire, and they would deflect. It became a dance we expertly performed over the years." She paused, her eyes momentarily distant as she remembered. "They passed away when I was in my early twenties, leaving me with more questions than answers. I had hoped that they might leave me with some clue, a hint as to where I came from. But their wills contained nothing of the sort. I want to believe that they didn't know either, that they, too, were kept in the dark about my origins, but..."

"But you think there's more to the story, don't you?"

"Yes," she replied, her eyes gleaming with determination. "I do. I mean no disrespect to my adoptive parents, but I want to know where I came from and who my birthparents were. What did they look like? What did their voices sound like? What was the color of my mother's eyes? I just need something— anything— to feel that connection."

"Have you tried searching for them? There must be records of your adoption somewhere."

Diane shook her head. "The records were sealed by the court. I've tried, trust me. Lawyers, private investigators... They've all looked into it, but no one has been able to tell me anything."

I had experienced my share of pain, but Diane's was a different kind of torment. She was in search of an identity that had been lulled to sleep, but never quite silenced.

"It's difficult to walk through life without knowing who you come from, without having that sense of continuity and connection. But my adoptive parents did their best, and in their own way, they gave me a wonderful life." After a long pause, she finished the last of her wine and said, "I think it's time for me to turn in for the night. It's late and we have a long day ahead of us tomorrow." She rose from the chair and gave me a crooked smile.

There was something in that smile, in the way one side of her mouth curled slightly more than the other, that seemed oddly familiar. The quirk was small, almost insignificant, but it caught my attention, nonetheless.

CHAPTER 21

Thursday

"Last night, I couldn't sleep, so I went through some old photo albums you had on the bookshelf," Diane said over breakfast the next morning. "I hope that was all right."

"Yes, of course."

Diane gave a relieved smile. "Good, because I was hoping to ask you a few questions." She spread out a photo album on the kitchen table, flipping through the pages until she found the picture she was looking for. It was a faded black and white photograph of three young women, all standing in front of the restaurant on the pier.

"This is you, isn't it?" she asked, pointing to the woman on the left.

"Yes, that's me," I said, smiling at the memories that picture stirred.

"And that's Judy?" she asked, pointing to the woman at the far right.

"Very good," I said, shocked that she had recognized her. Her hair was longer then, her face soft with youth.

"That must make this Rosalie," she surmised, indicating the woman in the center.

"Yes, that's Rosie," I said, a lump forming in my throat. I hadn't laid eyes on this picture in years, and the sight of her—

young, vibrant, full of life—pulled at a heartstring I thought had hardened over time.

"Can you tell me more about her?" Diane requested softly, her eyes studying the image. "For some reason, I feel this inexplicable pull toward her, as if she has some unfinished story to tell."

A chill rose the length of my spine, but I did my best to suppress it. I poured myself another cup of coffee and stared at the picture for a few seconds before I spoke. "That picture was taken a long time ago, about six months after I moved to Kitty Hawk. By then, the three of us had become good friends."

Kitty Hawk, NC

December 1962

"That's a wrap, girls," I said, shutting the door and flipping the sign to "Closed." We had just finished a particularly grueling shift. The holiday crowd had swarmed the restaurant that day, leaving us with little time to catch our breaths.

"What's the plan for tonight?" Judy asked, pulling off her apron and hanging it on the hook behind the door. Her eyes were twinkling with the anticipation of a night out.

"Well," I began, "we could head over to The Blue Lagoon. They've got a new band playing tonight."

Rosalie groaned and rolled her eyes. "Not another band. The last one you dragged us to was dreadful. I think I might stay in and write a little."

"Write? But it's Friday and the night is still young. I want to go out and do something fun."

Judy, ever the peacemaker, jumped in and suggested we try the movie theater in Manteo. "I think *Lawrence of Arabia* is playing. I'll even buy the popcorn."

It wasn't drinks and dancing, but it beat staying in, so I agreed.

* * *

The drive to Manteo was filled with laughter and light-hearted banter, the radio playing softly in the background as Judy navigated the winding roads. The three of us had become more than just coworkers. We were friends. In many ways, they had become the sisters I never had.

We reached the theater just in time for the opening credits, purchasing popcorn and sodas before settling into our seats. As the movie played out on the screen, I glanced over at Rosie and Judy from time to time, their faces illuminated by the flickering images. Rosie was lost in the story, her brow furrowed with an intensity that made me smile. Judy, on the other hand, was chewing her popcorn, her vacant gaze seemingly a thousand miles away. I knew she was probably thinking about Steve, the man from the gas station she'd been seeing.

As the movie reached its climactic end, I felt a strangely fitting sense of melancholy wash over me. Perhaps it was because I knew that these moments were fleeting, that the years would pass us by and our lives would become mere memories, or maybe it was just the inherent sadness of the film's story. I glanced at the girls, still engrossed in the movie, and felt a sudden surge of gratitude for their companionship. Without them, I didn't know where I would be.

When the movie ended, we shuffled out of the theater, each of us lost in our thoughts. The night air was cool and crisp, carrying with it the lingering scent of popcorn. We strolled down Main Street, past shuttered shops and empty diners, our footstep echoing in the quiet town.

"I think Peter might be the one," Rosie said as we crossed the street at the stop sign.

Judy laughed. "Good lord, Rosie, you can't be serious. You've only been going out for, what, a month?"

Rosie shrugged, her eyes staring straight ahead as she walked. "I know it sounds crazy, but I just have this feeling."

"You and your feelings," Judy said, reaching over to give Rosie a quick squeeze on the shoulder. "Just don't rush into anything, all right? I mean, Peter's a handsome guy and all, but you barely know him."

Rosie nodded, her gaze dropping to the pavement. "I know. I just... The fact of the matter is I'm not getting any younger, and I want to settle down. You know, build a life with someone."

"Then that's all that matters," I chimed in, hoping to lighten the mood. "Trust me, when you know, you know. And if you think Peter's the one, then who are we to tell you otherwise?"

If anyone knew about hasty decisions, it was me. My own past was riddled with impulsive choices. But I understood Rosie's longing for a life of stability and companionship.

"Thanks, Sara." She shot Judy a glance. "At least someone understands."

"I was only kidding," said Judy. "If you're happy, then I'm happy, too."

* * *

As the calendar flipped to January, the nights grew colder and our walks on the beach became less frequent. But our conversations about the future were unending. While Rosie focused on Peter and their budding romance, Judy and I were preoccupied with our own concerns. Despite having lived most of her life in Kitty Hawk, Judy was contemplating selling the restaurant and moving to New York to pursue her dream of becoming a chef. I, on the other hand, was still grappling with my unresolved feelings for Jack, wondering if I should reach out to him, or allow the wounds to heal on their own.

* * *

As time went on, I thought less of home and more of the life I was building in Kitty Hawk. My feelings for Jack still lingered in the back of my mind, but they were fading, like footprints washed away by the tide.

That spring, I joined a book club, something I had always wanted to do. A small step toward self-discovery, yes, but a significant one, nonetheless. And it was at this book club I met several more women about my age. As it turned out, we had more in common than just our love for books. They, too, had left their hometowns, some out of a need for adventure, but others to escape troubled pasts. The stories they shared about their old lives were harrowing, how they had lived under the shadow of an abusive father or a neglectful mother or both, how they had slept in bus shelters and under bridges before finally managing to piece their lives back together. The strength these women carried was inspiring, and I started to realize that if they could make it, so could I.

CHAPTER 22

Kitty Hawk, NC

June 1963

Over the next few months, Rosie and Peter's relationship flourished. They were seen all over town, strolling arm in arm through the park or having quiet dinners at some of the finest local restaurants. They even began attending church together, always sitting in the same pew near the back.

With Judy consumed with thoughts of Steve and her future, and Rosie enraptured by her blossoming love, I felt a little left out, a little lonely. I loved my friends and was genuinely happy for them, but their happiness only highlighted the absence of my own romantic interests. By most accounts, I was considered an old maid, having passed my thirty-first birthday without a husband or even the prospect of one.

But then one day, a curious thing happened, something that would alter the course of our lives forever.

* * *

It was just before dawn when I heard the sirens approaching. The high-pitched wail grew louder and louder, slicing through the quiet of the morning. I scrambled out of bed and rushed to the window, peering out onto the desolate beach below. Red lights painted the row houses in an eerie glow as two police cars pulled onto the beach.

No more than a hundred yards from my window, a body had washed ashore. It was a man, cold and lifeless, his face frozen with an expression of fear and shock. It took a few days, but eventually he was identified as Peter Sullivan, Rosie's boyfriend.

His death sent shockwaves through our little community, but no one felt them quite so strongly as Rosie. Judy and I did our best to console her, but the grief that shadowed her eyes deepened with each passing day. Her once warm brown eyes were replaced by a dull and distant stare, her smile a mere memory.

The weeks that followed were hard on all of us. Questions swirled, theories were tossed about, and every conversation seemed to revolve around the mysterious circumstances of Peter's death. But before anyone could piece together a plausible explanation, the police arrested Rosie and charged her with murder. The news of her arrest was like a bombshell. I couldn't believe what I was hearing. Rosie, sweet Rosie, who I had come to know and love, being accused of murder? The thought seemed preposterous. Yet the evidence against her was damning. They found Peter's watch in her purse, a handkerchief smeared with blood in her bedroom, and a letter that was interpreted as a threat against him.

Almost instantly, the town was divided. There were those, like me and Judy, who believed in Rosie's innocence, knowing that the sweet woman we knew could never be capable of such a horrendous act. But there were others, mostly men, who were quick to condemn her.

Being so close to the situation, I was drawn to the mystery, captivated by the unfolding drama more than I'd like to admit. The empty hours of my afternoons were filled with hushed conversations and speculation about Rosie's fate. And the more I heard, the more I was convinced that there was more to this story than met the eye.

In the ensuing weeks, I spent every free moment I had talking to anyone who would listen, gathering information, piecing together the facts of Peter's life and death. But there wasn't much to go on. Rosie had kept Peter at arm's length from me and Judy, making it hard to know who he really was, or what their relationship was like. Despite the lack of information, I was determined to uncover the truth.

Before I got carried away, Judy reminded me that I was no detective, and that poking my nose into other people's affairs was a dangerous game. She was right. I was no Sherlock Holmes. I was an ordinary woman who, until recently, had lived a very quiet life. So I decided to take a step back and let the professionals handle the case.

But my resolve didn't last long. One lazy afternoon, about a week before the trial began, a stranger walked into my life and rekindled that fire. He was an unassuming man, average height and build, with bright blue eyes that reminded me of the ocean. And he wore a smile that was equal parts charm and mystery.

"Miss," he said, settling onto a weathered wooden stool at the counter, "could I trouble you for a piece of apple pie and a cup of coffee?"

"Of course," I replied, mustering up a warm smile. It felt strained and foreign on my face, but it was sincere. That's something I vowed never to lose—sincerity, no matter how cold the world got. I brought him the pie and coffee, watching as he enjoyed each bite with a childlike enthusiasm. His simple joy was infectious, and I found myself smiling, a real, unforced smile.

"This pie... It's delicious," he said. "Did you make it yourself?"

"Yes. It's my mother's recipe," I said, a tinge of sorrow creeping in at the mention of her. "I'm glad you like it."

His face lit up. "Like it? I love it. Miss...?"

"Sara," I said, tucking a stray lock of hair behind my ear.

"Sara." He rolled the name on his tongue as if it were a sacred chant. "Well, Sara, this may be the best apple pie I've ever had."

The compliment was simple, yet it left a warm glow in my heart. His words were like a sudden splash of color on a drab canvas, brightening the mundanity of my day. "You're too kind, mister..."

"Andrew," he said, extending a hand. "Andrew Hastings." His grip was firm yet reassuring as I shook it lightly.

"Nice to meet you, Andrew," I said, pulling away and returning to the task of clearing the counter.

"The pleasure's all mine."

I could feel his eyes following me as I collected the dishes. There was something about him, about the way he looked at me, that made me feel seen in a way I hadn't in a long time. His gaze wasn't invasive or overbearing, but kind and appreciative—of my efforts, of me. It was equally refreshing and unsettling.

"What brings you to Kitty Hawk, Andrew?" I asked, returning with a fresh pot of coffee to offer him a refill. "Business or pleasure?"

"Business, actually," he said, accepting the refill with a nod.

"What kind of business?"

"I'm a lawyer. In fact, I'm the defense attorney for your friend, Rosalie Flores."

My heart gave a little lurch. "Really?" I gave him a closer look, noting his casual clothing and easygoing demeanor. There was nothing about him that screamed "defense attorney." "You don't look like an attorney."

He laughed lightly at that. "Thanks, I think. I find it much easier to do my job when people don't realize I'm doing it."

I raised an eyebrow at his candidness. "You certainly had me fooled. Let's just hope you're as good at your job as you are concealing it, because my friend is innocent, and she needs a lawyer that can prove it."

He gave a wry smile. "Trust me, Sara, I'm very good at what I do." There was a confidence in his voice that was assuring, though I wasn't quite ready to trust him with Rosie's fate. "There it is," I said, leaning against the counter. "That lawyer ego I'm familiar with."

He laughed again. "Guilty as charged. You seem to know us quite well. Let me guess, you're related to someone in the business?"

I shook my head. "No, but I once had aspirations of becoming a lawyer myself."

His brows shot up in surprise. "Really? What changed your mind?"

I shrugged. "When I was younger, I had this fear of speaking in public. The thought of standing in front of a courtroom, all eyes on me, made my stomach churn. But over the years, I've outgrown that fear, found my voice. I only wish I'd found it sooner."

He gave me an understanding smile. "It's never too late, you know."

I smiled wistfully. "I'm sure you're right, but I'm happy here, for now. More coffee?"

"Sure." He slid his cup across the counter. As I filled it, he steered the conversation in a different direction. "Would it surprise you to know that most of the people I've talked to around here seem to think Rosalie did it?"

I frowned, my hands gripping the coffee pot a little tighter. "No, but that's because they don't know Rosie the way we do. Me and Judy, that is." I gestured in her direction. "Judy owns this place, and Rosie and I work for her. I've heard the rumors, that Rosie was upset because she found out Peter was cheating on her, but she wouldn't throw away her life over some man's foolishness. She has too much to lose, like her dream of becoming a nurse."

"I've seen people throw away their lives for less," Andrew replied with a casual shrug. "But I believe you, Sara. I don't know Rosie like you do, of course, but I don't believe she murdered anyone."

"You don't?"

"Of course not. I wouldn't have taken the case if I thought she did it. Besides, I've spoken to Rosalie. I've seen the evidence. And something doesn't quite add up."

Not that it changed anything, but it was comforting to know that someone else was on our side.

"Does that mean you can help her?"

"I'm going to try my best," he said, his gaze earnest and steady. "That's a promise."

Hope flickered in my chest. For the first time since Rosie's arrest, I felt a weight lift off my shoulders. After tending to some of my regulars, I returned to the counter and asked Andrew where he was from and how he had learned of the case.

"Atlanta," he answered with a slight drawl. "I received a call from Paula Fox, one of my dearest friends. She expressed some doubts about the public defender's ability to try this case. Paula knows I have a knack for these types of situations, so she reached out to me."

I knew Paula well. She and her husband frequented the restaurant and always sat at the same table. She'd mentioned having a famous lawyer friend once, but I never imagined I'd meet him, or that he'd be here to help Rosie."

"This place must be quite a change for you then if you come from Atlanta. It's a far cry from the big city."

"You could say that," he agreed, glancing out the window at the ocean. "But it isn't an unpleasant one. The pace here is calming and the view...stunning," he said, bringing his eyes back to me. "Yes, I could definitely get used to a place like this."

I smiled at his appreciation for our little town. "To be honest, it took me some time to adjust as well."

"You're not from here either?"

I shook my head. "Moved here about a year ago...from Tennessee."

"Tennessee, eh?" He gave a nod of approval. "I spent a little time up there a few years back. What part are you from?"

"East Tennessee...around Knoxville."

"Ah, Knoxville," he mused, his gaze becoming distant. "I have a cousin that lives in Knoxville. That's a lovely part of the country. The lakes, the mountains. I considered moving there myself, once. So why'd you leave such a beautiful place?"

The question had been asked before, by nearly everyone I'd met. But this felt different, like he was genuinely interested in the answer.

"I was tired of chasing after dreams that would never come

true," I admitted, shocked at my own candor. "So I left."

He gave an understanding nod, swirling the last of the coffee in his cup. "Well," he said, checking his watch, "I hate to eat and run, but I'm afraid duty calls." He slid off the stool and reached into the pocket of his jacket, producing a handful of bills which he laid on the counter. "But thank you —for the delicious pie and the conversation. This has been...helpful."

I nodded, my fingers brushing over the crisp bills as I mentally calculated the tip. "Any time."

"Will you be here tomorrow?" he asked as he pivoted toward the door.

I nodded and he gave me a lopsided grin. "Good. In that case, I'll see you then."

* * *

When we had closed up for the night, Judy and I sat down at the bar and ate our dinner. We were quiet. The words exchanged earlier with Andrew filled my thoughts. The restaurant was different when it was empty, like a stage after the actors have gone home. It had a certain hollowness that could only be filled by patrons.

"Who was that man I saw you talking to earlier?" Judy asked, eyebrows arched in curiosity.

"Rosie's lawyer...Andrew Hastings."

"Andrew," she repeated, her eyes narrowing slightly as she chewed her lip. "He seemed quite taken with you."

"Seriously? We were just talking."

Judy smirked. "Just talking, huh? That's how it always starts." She popped a fry into her mouth, grinning at me over her plate.

I rolled my eyes at her but couldn't suppress the smile that tugged at my lips. "I highly doubt getting to know a waitress at a random restaurant in the middle of nowhere is at the top of his priorities list. Besides, he's here on business."

Judy took her plate to the sink and rinsed it off. When she returned, her playful expression was gone, replaced by a more serious one. "Did he give you any indication that he would be able to help Rosie?"

I paused, my mind replaying our conversation. "He seemed hopeful, but he also said it wouldn't be easy. That he'd seen guilty verdicts with far less evidence."

Judy nodded, her gaze lingering on the empty tables before she spoke again. "We can only hope he knows what he's doing, and that Rosie will be okay. Otherwise, we're all going to be in for a very rough time."

CHAPTER 23

The next day, as promised, Andrew was back. He walked into the restaurant and took up the same seat as the day before, a small grin appearing when he saw me. As I served him a lunch of fried fish and hushpuppies, he told me stories about the places he'd been, the things he'd done, and the people he'd met were mesmerizing, painting a picture of a life lived to the fullest.

In between taking orders and pouring drinks, I told Andrew about Sims Chapel, the people I knew, and my years spent teaching. He listened attentively, his gaze never wavering from my face, as if every word I said was the most fascinating thing he'd ever heard.

"What about you—did you always know you wanted to be a lawyer?"

"Not exactly. Actually, I wanted to be a painter when I was younger. But life took me down a different path."

"A painter, huh? Like, houses?"

"No, like Van Gogh, Monet."

"Oh. That's different. Were you any good at it?"

He chuckled at that, dabbing the corners of his mouth with the napkin. "I was decent, I suppose. But I knew I would never be great. And I wanted to be great."

"For what it's worth, I think you chose the right career. After you left yesterday, I called Paula and asked her about you. She had nothing but good things to say. She also said that you've never lost a case. Is that true?"

A blush crept up his neck, and he glanced down at his half-eaten plate of food. "It is."

"Impressive. Tell me, how does it feel to stand before a courtroom and argue a case? To fight for what you believe is right?"

"Intense," he said, his eyes distant as if he was reliving the experiences. "Like you're locked in a battle of words and wit. Every argument is a bullet, every rebuttal a shield. The adrenaline, the thrill of a well-made point...intoxicating."

"You certainly paint a vivid picture," I said, smiling at his description. "After we spoke yesterday, I wondered if I had made the right choice in becoming a teacher. My mind wandered to what could have been if I had chosen law instead of mathematics."

"And what did you conclude?"

"That I may have missed my calling. That doesn't mean I regret the path I chose. Touching the lives of young minds, inspiring them to make a difference in the world, is a reward like no other. But..."

He considered this for a moment, swirling the last of his coffee in his cup. "I suppose there's always a part of us that wonders, isn't there? The road not taken and all that. You know, I did some thinking, too, after we spoke."

"Oh?" I leaned in. "What about?"

"If my defense of Rosalie is to be successful, I'm going to need some help. Believe it or not, preparing for trial is not just about me, it's a team effort, and right now I'm a team of one."

"I'm not sure I follow."

He looked up at me with a serious expression, the playful glint gone from his eyes. "I need someone who can help gather information critical to the case, sort through evidence, that sort of thing. Someone with an analytical mind, who can make connections where others may not. Someone like you. Unfortunately, I can't compensate you due to your friendship with the defendant, but it would be a great opportunity for you to work on a real case, see if it's something that interests you."

His offer caught me off guard. "I—I don't know what to say. Don't you already have someone that does those things for you?"

"Normally, yes, but she recently moved, and I've been struggling to find a temporary replacement. I know I'm going out on a limb here, but I think you'd be perfect for the job."

I hesitated, mulling over his proposition. It was an incredible opportunity, one most people would jump at. But was I really prepared for something like this? "I'm flattered, really, but I wouldn't know where to start. Plus, I couldn't possibly compare to your previous assistant."

He leaned back, regarding me with a steady gaze. "True, but everyone starts somewhere. My assistant was also very green when she started, but she quickly learned the ropes. Tell you what, sleep on it before you give me an answer. Opening statements start in a few days, so why don't you come down to the courthouse and see how things work? If it seems like something you're interested in, we can talk more. If not, no hard feelings. How does that sound?"

Andrew's world seemed so different from mine, thrilling and intimidating all at once. My hesitance must have shown on my face, because he quickly followed his offer with a reassuring smile.

"All right," I said, finding myself agreeing to his invitation. "I'll do it. I'll come down to the courthouse and check it out.

But just so we're clear, I'm not making any commitment beyond that."

CHAPTER 24

"Sara, wake up. Today's the big day." The sound of Judy's voice echoed down the hall, bouncing off the low ceiling and worn floorboards.

"I'm up," came my reply, muffled by a heaping pile of quilts.

"You've got to get a move on," Judy called again as she burst through the door. She pulled back the faded floral curtains, allowing the early morning sunshine to creep into the room. "Andrew will be by to get you soon, and you don't want to keep him waiting."

The quilts stirred as I pushed myself up, my brown hair wild and knotted. "I know," I said, rubbing the sleep from my eyes. "I just wish I'd slept better." I'd had a dream where I was back home in Tennessee, sitting at the water's edge. In the dream, there were no trials to fret over. Only the serenity of the lake and the soft whisper of the wind in the trees. "Sometimes, it feels so real, like I never left."

"I know," Judy said softly, smoothing away a few errant strands of hair from my forehead. "Now, splash some water on your face and get dressed. Your clothes are on a hanger in the closet and breakfast is on the table downstairs."

With a nod, I pulled myself out of the quilts, my legs shaking slightly as they landed on the cool wooden floor. My bare feet padded across the room toward the small closet, the boards creaking slightly under my weight. Grabbing the hanger, I felt the smooth fabric of my dress, the green one with the pleats that tied at the waist. A pair of nude heels sat below the dress, their familiar touch a small comfort.

Judy quietly left the room, allowing me privacy as I dressed. I pulled the dress over my head, the fabric falling into place around my slender frame. I took a moment to smooth out the wrinkles in the soft sunlight filtering through the window. I slipped on the heels, wobbling a bit as my body adjusted to their height.

Once I had combed out my hair and put on my makeup, I came downstairs for breakfast.

The smell of freshly brewed coffee and bacon filled the restaurant, creating a comforting warmth that eased some of my anxiety. Judy was in the kitchen, her back turned to the table as she dished scrambled eggs onto a plate.

"You look lovely," Judy said over her shoulder. "Very professional."

"Thanks."

"Here, eat." She set down the plate of eggs and a steaming mug of coffee in front of me. "So, will you be at the courthouse all day?"

"I'm not sure. Andrew said usually opening arguments are brief, but I guess we'll see. Either way, I'm just there to observe, to see if it's something I'm interested in." I took a sip of the coffee. The warm liquid slid down my throat and spread through my body, waking up my senses and helping me feel a little more grounded.

"I see," Judy responded. "Well, if it is something you want to do, don't worry about things here. I'm capable of holding hold down the fort on my own."

"Thanks. I was worried about that."

"Do you think Andrew is nervous?" Judy asked.

"Doubt it. This is his playground. Besides, I reckon he thrives under pressure. Says it makes him feel alive."

"That's good." The corners of her lips inched up into a minuscule smile. "For Rosie's sake, I mean."

By the time Andrew knocked on the door, I was feeling a bit more composed. At the sound of his knock, I took a deep breath and swung open the door.

"Morning," Andrew said with a tight-lipped smile. "Are you ready to go?"

"As ready as I'll ever be."

"Good," he said, patting my shoulder gently. "Today should be quite the experience. Remember, just observe. Nothing more."

With that final piece of advice, we stepped outside and were greeted by the bright morning sun, already beating down with a heat that promised an uncomfortably hot day. Andrew pulled out a handkerchief, mopping his brow before he even made it to the car.

"Good grief," he muttered, squinting against the sun's glare. "Looks like it's going to be a scorcher."

I followed him, eyes lowered to avoid the harsh light. The humidity seeped through my clothing, making me wish I had opted for something a little less formal.

As he headed south along the coast, Andrew advised me to focus on the jurors. "They're the most important piece of this whole thing. Watch their faces, their body language. Your feedback will help me judge whether or not I need to change tactics."

I nodded at his instructions, focusing on his words as a distraction from my nervous thoughts. Andrew continued talking, outlining the expected order of events and what his strategy would be. I instinctively reached for the pen and pad I'd brought along, jotting down the key points as he spoke.

We arrived at the courthouse amidst a flurry of activity. Reporters descended upon us, like a swarm of locusts bearing down on a fresh crop.

"Remember to keep your head down and don't say anything to the press," Andrew cautioned, his tone serious now.

I nodded, pushing my nerves aside as best as I could. The sea of reporters, their flashing cameras, and insistent queries were daunting, but Andrew's confident strides through the swarming mass reassured me. He was a rock amid a stormy sea, unyielding and steadfast, and I clung to that stability as we made our way to the entrance of the building.

Inside, the polished marble floors and grand pillars cast an imposing atmosphere. The quiet murmur of other lawyers, bailiffs, and judges echoed through the high-ceilinged hall, interspersed with the clicking heels of those passing by. I felt a shiver snake its way up my spine as we made our way to the courtroom.

"You sit here," Andrew instructed, offering me a seat in the front row. "And remember, just observe."

I nodded, taking a seat on the pew. Andrew took his place at the defendant's table, shuffling through his papers and organizing them on the desk in front of him.

Rosie was led into the courtroom next, a bailiff at her side. As the crowd filed in and filled the pews, an eerie hush fell over the room. All eyes were on Rosie. She wore a simple navy dress and a serene expression that bore no trace of the fear she must have been feeling. I gave her a small wave, whispering, "It'll be all right."

"All rise." The bailiffs booming voice reverberated around the room, causing everyone to stand. When Judge Howard Slocolm entered the room, the tension seemed to intensify. He was an imposing figure, with a stern countenance and eyes that seemed to pierce into one's very soul. I dared not look him in the eyes. His robes billowed as he took his seat behind the bench, an unspoken signal for everyone else to follow suit.

The judge began to read out the charges against Rosie, his voice cool and measured. "Rosalie Flores, you are here on charges of murder in the first degree. How do you plead?"

Rosie swallowed hard, her gaze on the judge. "Not guilty, Your Honor."

A shocked murmur rippled through the courtroom. I nodded in Rosie's direction, offering a supportive smile.

"Very well," Judge Slocolm said, then nodded at the prosecutor. "Is the state ready to proceed?"

The prosecutor, a man named Arthur Gentry, rose from his seat. He was a rather tall man with slicked-back hair and a predatory smile. "Ready, Your Honor," he began with a smooth voice that seemed to seep into every nook of the courtroom. "We are prepared to prove beyond a reasonable doubt that Ms. Flores is guilty of the crime for which she stands accused. As you will see from the evidence and testimonies, Ms. Flores not only had motive and opportunity, but she left a damning trail of evidence that screams out her guilt." He turned toward the defense table and smirked. "Mr. Hastings will try to convince you otherwise, but I ask you not to be swayed by his smoke and mirrors."

In response, Andrew rose, his expression one of calm assurance. "Your Honor," he began in a voice much softer than Gentry's, his tone steady and sincere. "I stand here today not with smoke and mirrors, but with the truth. A truth that will prove Rosalie Flores to be innocent of these vile accusations." Without breaking his calm demeanor, he turned to the jury and his gaze swept over them. "Ladies and gentlemen of the jury, truth is not always what it appears. And in this case, the truth is far from what the prosecution would have you believe. A truth that has been shaped by an intricate web of deception and manipulation. A truth that is, at its heart, centered on a harmless woman wrongly accused of an act she could not possibly have committed." He paused for dramatic effect before focusing once again on the jury. "We'll prove to you that this is a case of mistaken identity. A case of a vindictive smear campaign against an innocent woman driven by hidden agendas and personal vendettas." His voice had a soothing cadence that washed over the courtroom, softening the harshness of Gentry's accusation.

"But I ask you," he continued, turning toward the Judge, "to keep an open mind through these proceedings. To remember that, here in this room, the cornerstone of our justice system— innocent until proven guilty—prevails."

Sitting back down, he allowed his words to linger in the quiet that followed. Across the room, Gentry's smile didn't falter. He wore it like a man who had seen hundreds of defendants come and go—defeated, broken under his watchful eye. Yet Andrew seemed undeterred.

At half past four, the court adjourned for the day, leaving everyone in suspense. The discussion buzzed in subdued whispers as people filed out of the courtroom. Rosie was led away, her face impassive but her tired eyes reflecting the strain of the day.

"So, what did you think?" he asked as he gathered his papers into a neat stack and placed them in his briefcase.

"I think you've got your work cut out for you. I'm no lawyer, but the prosecution seems to have a strong case. I saw the jurors nodding while Mr. Gentry spoke. Are you sure you didn't bite off more than you can chew?"

He chuckled, running a hand through his hair. "I like a challenge," he said, his eyes gleaming with determination. "Besides, I believe in her. More importantly, I believe in her innocence." He shut his briefcase and pulled his coat from the back of the chair, shrugging into it. "And if there's one thing I've learned in this profession," he continued as he led me out into the hallway, "it's that things are rarely as they seem."

We took the service elevator to the basement and exited into the parking lot, avoiding the crowd. The hot air hit us like a wall, but Andrew didn't flinch.

"So, was it what you were expecting?"

"Considering it's the first trial I've ever been to, I'm not sure what I was expecting. But it was certainly intense."

"Trials tend to be that way. And, if you don't mind me asking, how would you rate my performance?"

"You certainly seemed to hold your own against Mr. Gentry. By the way, I don't like that man. He's very smug."

Andrew chuckled. "Arthur's not a bad man. He's just doing his job. By the way, thank you," he said as we came to a stop near his black sedan, "for being here today. It means a lot that you were here and that you stepped outside your comfort zone."

"You're welcome. Believe it or not, I rather enjoyed myself today. Who knew courtrooms could be so thrilling?"

"I'm glad," he said as he opened the door and put his briefcase in the passenger seat. "I might be way off, but it sounds as if you're leaning toward helping me."

"Maybe," I responded with a sly grin.

And with that, he threw me a smirk before opening the car door for me.

* * *

"Listen," he said as he dropped me off in front of the pier, "I have to meet with Rosalie now, but would you like to grab dinner later? That is, if you don't have plans. I'd like to further discuss the assistant role."

"Maybe," I said again, drawing out the word teasingly.

"Then maybe I'll pick you up at seven."

I watched as he drove away, his shiny black sedan disappearing into the distance. Standing there, I couldn't help but admire his confidence, his determination. Despite the odds stacked against him, and the public scrutiny he was under, he carried himself with a grace that was both captivating and reassuring. And although I knew he was only in town for a short time, I wanted to get to know him better.

Later that evening, I paced restlessly as I tried to decide what to wear to our dinner. I threw open my closet, staring at the options. Nothing seemed right for this dinner date. Eventually, I settled on a simple floral dress, hoping to appear as calm and collected as he always did. As the hours slipped away, my anticipation grew. I was nervous, excited, and unsure all at once, but I was ready for whatever the evening would bring.

At precisely seven o'clock, Andrew's car pulled up and I went out to meet him. He had already stepped out of the car, leaning casually against the vehicle with a broad grin on his face. He looked different in the evening light, softer somehow. His suit had been replaced with a simple pair of blue slacks and a casual shirt, making him appear less like the high-powered attorney I had seen in the courtroom, and more like the charming, approachable man I hoped he was.

"You look lovely," he said, holding the car door open for me.

"Thank you. You don't look so bad yourself."

The restaurant Andrew chose was a quiet, intimate place a few blocks up from the pier. Lit by warm, flickering candlelight and filled with the soft rustle of conversation, it felt worlds away from the cold, clinical courthouse we had left earlier.

We were led to a secluded corner table where we could talk freely without being overheard.

"Is this all right?" he asked, gently pulling out my chair.

"Yes, it's perfect."

Andrew's eyes crinkled at the corners as he smiled. We ordered our food and, while waiting, slipped into a conversation that flowed as easily as the wine. He spoke of his childhood in a small town in Georgia, his journey to law school, and the cases that had shaped his career. In between, he asked me about my life. I opened up to him in ways I hadn't anticipated, sharing bits and pieces of my past that I'd kept tucked away, even from my closest friends. Like the time I snuck into the mathematics department at midnight during my college years to solve an equation that had been left unfinished on the chalkboard, or the summer I spent learning to speak French, hoping that one day, I'd visit Paris and converse with the locals without stumbling over words. Andrew listened intently, his eyes never leaving mine, making me feel heard in a way I had rarely experienced.

Our meal arrived but was almost forgotten as we delved deeper into each other's lives. As the evening wore on, we found ourselves sharing laughter and stories, our lives intertwining with each anecdote. The noise around us faded to a mere whisper as our own dialogue took center stage. He had a way of making me feel like the only person in the room, his full attention completely focused on each word I uttered.

"Now that we're properly acquainted," he said, leaning back in his chair and regarding me with a thoughtful expression, "what's the real reason you left Tennessee?"

I thought about lying, about creating some bland excuse about needing a change of scenery or seeing a new opportunity, but if my past had taught me anything it was that honesty was essential. "I left because someone broke my heart," I said, looking down at the remnants of food on my plate. "Someone I cared for deeply, and I couldn't stand the thought of being there anymore."

Andrew nodded, understanding etched in his eyes. "I'm sorry you had to go through that."

"Not as sorry as I am." I spent the next few minutes explaining to Andrew my role in the demise of that relationship. How my jealousy and lies had driven away the one person I cared about. As the words poured out of me, I felt a weight lift from my shoulders, a sense of liberation that came from acknowledging my past mistakes. "And that's why I moved here," I concluded. "Hoping for a fresh start."

"You know, sometimes it's the broken pieces that make us who we are," said Andrew. "Take me, for example. I've had my heart broken more times than I care to admit, but I keep putting myself out there, hoping that the next one is the one I've been waiting for."

His eyes bore into mine, their intensity reflecting the sincerity of his words. Despite myself, I felt a spark of hope ignite within me. Was it possible that I could find love again after all the mistakes I had made?

"So, the legal assistant job," I said, changing the subject.

"I've given it a great deal of thought, and I have decided to accept your offer, under one condition."

"And what might that be?"

"That you're patient with me. When it comes to this world, I'm a fish out of water, and I'm going to need time to adjust. I can't promise that I'll be perfect or that I won't make mistakes, but I can assure you that I will try my best every single day."

"Patience is something I can certainly afford," he said as he reached across the table, extending a hand to me. "And I think you're selling yourself short. Something tells me you're far more capable than you give yourself credit for."

"In that case," I said, giving his hand a firm shake, "You've got yourself a deal."

CHAPTER 25

Present

"Is that when you knew you wanted to be a lawyer?" Diane asked as she looked up from her notepad.

I shook my head. "No, that came later. When I first agreed to take the job as Andrew's assistant, I was terrified. I had no experience dealing with the police, courts, or anything of the sort. Part of me thought that Andrew was crazy for soliciting my help. But all I kept thinking about was poor Rosie. I thought if I could make a difference, even a small one, it would be worth it."

"And did you?" Diane asked. "Make a difference?"

I tipped my head in a nod. "Not at first. It took me a little while to get my feet wet."

At noon, we broke for lunch, enjoying Cobb salads and sweet tea on the veranda. We talked about the case and my first stumbling steps into the world of law. When we'd finished eating, Diane told me more about her life as a journalist and how she'd gotten into the profession.

"I've always wanted to be a writer," she said as she cleaned her glasses on the hem of her blouse. "Even as a little girl, I'd scribble stories in my notebooks. Later, I realized I had a knack for asking questions—the right questions—and that's when journalism became a possibility."

"How long have you been an investigative journalist?"

"Five years next month."

"And do you enjoy it?"

"I do, but I still dream of becoming a novelist. This story of yours will certainly help me on my journey, but I want to write my own stories, you know? The kind that touches people's hearts and stays with them long after they've put the book down."

"Does that mean you want to try your hand at fiction?"

She nodded, a faraway look in her eyes. "Yes, but not just any fiction. I want to write stories that inspire people, give them hope, make them see the world a little differently. Actually, if I'm being totally honest, I want to write the next great American novel. I hope you don't take offense to that."

I laughed under my breath. "Not at all, dear. I love fiction as much as anyone. And your desire to write the next great American novel reminds me of someone I used to know," I said, thinking of Jack. "But I will say this—the old adage that truth can be stranger than fiction—it's very true, so don't write off nonfiction just yet."

We both chuckled at the irony and the conversation took a lighter turn. Over cups of coffee, Diane and I continued building a friendship. Through the afternoon, our discussions meandered through politics, literature, and our shared love for nature and more specifically, the ocean. Diane also told me more about Cassie and how she had recently gotten a puppy, a chocolate Maltipoo she had affectionately named Rolo, after her favorite candy.

As the afternoon wore on, the sun sank lower in the western sky, setting the horizon aflame. Before dinner, we retreated to our respective rooms. Diane needed time to compile her notes, and I needed time to reflect on the day's conversation, breathing in the poignant solitude that often came with dusk.

Judy joined me before dinner, and we watched the sunset together.

"How are things going with Diane?" she asked as she gazed out toward the beach.

"Quite well. She's an interesting young woman."

Judy smiled, her delicate features illuminated by the soft glow of the porch light. "I'm glad to hear it."

"You know, she reminds me a little bit of Rosie."

"Rosie? Really?"

"Not so much in the physical appearance, but in her spirit, her mannerisms. Not to mention her passion for writing."

Judy smiled at the memory. Rosie had been a whirlwind, filling our lives with energy and her love for words.

"Maybe it's only fitting that Diane is here then," Judy mused out loud. "Perhaps fate has a way of circling back and reminding us of what we once cherished."

"And maybe reminding us of what we can still cherish," I said as the sun went down.

Since we'd taken a break from the hard-hitting questions to talk about our personal lives, Diane and I continued our conversation after dinner. Normally, I would have called it a night, but considering Diane was only with me for two more days, and there was still so much to tell, I had to push the story along.

Kitty Hawk, NC

June 1963

Day two of the trial began with a sunrise as murky as the evidence against Rosie. The courthouse was packed again with spectators, some there to support her, others simply devouring the spectacle. The jury sat at attention, each face betraying a different interpretation of the evidence. The gavel crashed down, marking the start of the proceedings.

The prosecutor paced in front of the jury box, his stride methodical and predatory, keeping the room on the edge of their seats. Every now and then he would stop abruptly, pivot sharply on his heel and thrust a damning piece of evidence toward the jury.

That was the moment I realized just how difficult the road ahead would be for Andrew in his defense of Rosie. But despite the seemingly insurmountable odds, Andrew never wavered. He was not a man of impressive stature like Mr. Gentry, nor did he have an icy stare that could pierce your very soul. Instead, his eyes were warm and kind, his body language relaxed yet assertive. He had an air about him that made you feel at ease, as if everything would be all right.

In my search for evidence to aid Rosie's defense, I began by delving deeper into Peter's past. Having only met him a few times, I didn't know him that well. But there was one detail that stuck out in my memory. He had mentioned having a beachside cottage in nearby Nags Head, so I decided to start there.

I made the short drive from Kitty Hawk to Nags Head with the windows down, losing myself in my thoughts. The coastal winds rumbled around me, whipping my hair into a frizz. As I arrived at the cottage, a quaint little structure painted blue and white, I felt a twinge of uncertainty. Perhaps it was the eerie quietness that hung around the place or the way the salty air seemed heavier, but something gave me pause.

Getting out of the car, I shook the feeling off and began my investigation.

"You looking for something, Miss?" a voice called out as I stepped onto the porch.

I turned to see an elderly man with a weathered face and keen eyes, staring at me from the driveway. His posture was relaxed, yet his gaze was intense, as if he knew something I didn't.

"I'm trying to find out more about the man who lived here," I said, trying to sound casual. "Peter Sullivan. Did you know him?"

The old man's eyes narrowed slightly at the mention of the name, his face weathering into a deep frown. "Yeah, I knew him...or at least I knew of him. He wasn't much for conversation. Mostly kept to himself."

I nodded, hiding my disappointment. "Did he ever have any visitors? Anyone you can remember?"

"Now that you mention it, there was this one woman. She'd come by every now and then, mostly on the weekends."

I stepped off the porch, producing a picture of Rosie and showing it to the man. "Was it her?"

He shook his head immediately. "No, that's the young lady accused of killing Peter. She came by only once or twice. The girl I'm thinking of was different. She was a redhead. Always wore sunglasses and had this look about her, like she was ashamed to be seen."

A redhead? I hadn't seen anything about a redhead in the

case files. Could this be the woman Peter was seeing behind Rosie's back? "Do you remember her name?"

He hesitated, rubbing his stubbled chin thoughtfully. "Can't say that I do," he admitted, his brow creasing in concentration. "Peter didn't introduce us, and she wasn't one for chit-chat."

"Anything else you remember about her?" I pressed, grasping for at any information that might start to untangle this web.

"Can't say much beyond what I've already told ya," the old man said, looking somewhat apologetic. "She'd usually show up in the evenings, stay for a few hours and then vanish like the tide. And...yeah, there was something else." He paused, as if weighing his words carefully. "She always drove this old blue Cadillac. Must've been from the fifties. Beautiful car, but it stuck out like a sore thumb."

An old blue Cadillac. That was something at least, even if it was a thin lead to follow.

"Thank you," I said, offering him a grateful smile. "You've been very helpful."

He simply nodded, resuming his stroll. With nothing more to gain, I turned away from the house and headed back to my car. As I maneuvered down the winding coastal roads, the mystery of Peter Sullivan, and his mysterious redhead, deepened.

* * *

I met up with Andrew at a diner in Manteo, where we could discuss the case without the prying ears and eyes of the townsfolk. He waited for me at a corner booth, his face buried in the local newspaper when I walked in.

"Any luck?" he asked as I slid into the red vinyl booth

opposite him.

"Sort of. I've got a new lead, but I'm not sure how much it's worth."

Andrew lowered his newspaper, his brow lifted in curiosity. "Oh?"

I told him about the old man and the mysterious redhead with her blue Cadillac.

"That's a start," he said, folding the newspaper and setting it aside. "Could be a mistress, could be a close friend. Either way, we need to find this woman. She might know more about Peter's actions leading up to his death."

The waitress appeared then and took our orders. After taking a sip of my Coke, I looked up at Andrew and asked, "Do you think it would be possible for Judy and me to see Rosie? We haven't spoken to her since her arrest, and we want her to know we haven't forgotten her."

"I think that can be arranged. Just remember, they'll probably be listening to everything you say, so choose your words carefully."

Our food arrived, and we ate in relative silence. When we had filled our stomachs, we began to discuss our plan of action.

"All right," Andrew began, folding his napkin meticulously onto his empty plate. "I'll contact the prison tomorrow and arrange for you and Judy to meet with Rosalie. Since it's the weekend, we have a couple of days to gather evidence, and I want to find out who this woman is that Peter was spotted with. In the meantime, I want you to look into that blue Cadillac. It's not a common car around here, so someone must know something about it. And if there's time, I want to retrace Rosalie's steps the night of the murder. Maybe there's something we missed."

When we got back to the pier, Andrew parked the car

and we talked for a while—about the case, about what he expected from me in the coming weeks, and about ourselves. We sat there, listening to the waves in the distance, enjoying each other's company. Underneath the soft glow of moonlight, Andrew turned to me, his face partially obscured by shadows. I could still make out his eyes, though. They were warm, filled with a gentle sincerity that made my heart flutter.

"I have a confession to make," he said. "You asked me once if I had ever lost a case, remember?"

I nodded, recalling our conversation.

"And I told you I hadn't. Well, that wasn't entirely true. I have lost a case before, just one, but not as a defense attorney. When my career began, I was working for the district attorney's office in Atlanta as a prosecutor. I always thought convicting the bad guys was my calling, but I quickly discovered that it wasn't as black-and-white as I had initially thought. It never dawned on me that sometimes innocent people were charged with crimes. I was young...green...ambitious. There was this man... James Kellerman. He was accused of a robbery gone wrong, a convenience store clerk ended up dead. The evidence against Kellerman was flimsy at best, but I didn't see it then. I was too focused on winning the case, making a name for myself."

His voice dropped to barely more than a whisper, tinged with regret. "Anyway, a couple of days before the trial ended, I discovered evidence that had been suppressed by the DA's office, evidence that would have cleared Kellerman. I reported what I found, but the DA didn't want a mistrial. He wanted a conviction."

"What did you do?"

"The only thing I could do. I revealed the evidence to the judge and the defense team, and then I quit."

"That's quite a story," I said, having completely misjudged him. I'd seen him as a slick lawyer, playing the game, always on the winning side. But this revelation painted him in a new light. He was a man of principle, willing to risk his career for justice. "That must have been hard, thinking you wanted to go one direction, only to find out that it was the wrong path."

"Yes and no," said Andrew. "On the one hand, I felt as if I'd wasted time. But on the other, I discovered a new purpose, a new direction."

That's when it dawned on me that Andrew and I were more alike than I initially thought. He, too, had spent years chasing something he thought he wanted, only to realize that it wasn't what he truly desired. I could see in his eyes that he was a man who had experienced the bitter taste of disillusionment, just as I had. "How did you become a defense attorney?" I asked, curious about the transition.

"After the Kellerman case," he began, shifting in his seat, "I took some time off to clear my head, reassess my priorities. I traveled for a bit, visited places I'd never seen before. During that time, I did a lot of soul-searching. That was when I realized the kind of lawyer I wanted to be. I wanted to be the one who defended the underdog, who took on the hard cases, not just the ones that were easy to win. I wanted to ensure that justice was served, no matter what."

The passion in his voice was palpable, a far cry from the calculated coolness he displayed in the courtroom. His shift in career, although subtle, had been not just a professional transformation but also a personal one.

"You know, I'm really glad you decided to join me on this journey. I wasn't sure how we would work together, given our different backgrounds. But I'm beginning to see that our diverse backgrounds can really complement each other."

"Me too," I said, surprised at the sincerity in my voice. "I was nervous that I'd be in over my head, that I'd be out of place in your world."

Andrew looked at me, spearing me with his gaze. "Believe me, you're exactly where you need to be."

Without saying another word, he leaned forward, closing the distance between us. I felt drawn to him, the magnetic pull between us undeniable. But before our lips could meet, I pulled back, a sudden surge of doubt flooding my thoughts.

"Did I do something wrong?" he asked, his face twisted in confusion.

"No. You've done everything right. It's just... This has all been so fast, so unexpected. I'm not sure if I'm ready. Plus, we work together. Not to mention, you're only here for a short time and I don't want to get used to something that's not permanent." My voice was a little more vulnerable than I had intended. Andrew pulled back and took a breath. It was a small move, but it seemed to create a chasm between us. His eyes, a moment ago filled with warmth and understanding, were now guarded and distant.

"I understand," he said quietly. "Is there any chance we could forget about what just happened? I really enjoy your company, and I don't want that ruined by my impulsiveness."

I thought about it. His earnestness was touching, his words sincere. I had felt a connection with Andrew, one that was rare, something I hadn't experienced in a long time. But it was this very connection that scared me. "Of course. I enjoy being around you, too. And don't worry, you didn't ruin anything."

After Andrew drove away, I went to my room and stared at my reflection in the window, wondering if I should have kissed him. His words played over and over in my mind, and I could see a hint of something different in my eyes. Hope, maybe? Or was it denial? Was I fooling myself into believing I could have a second chance at love?

I sat on the edge of my bed, tracing the floral pattern on my bedspread. Memories flitted through my mind, a cascade of moments that had led me to this point. I remembered the anguish, the heartbreak, but also the resilience and strength I had discovered within myself. Since arriving in Kitty Hawk, I had been piecing myself back together, learning to carry the weight of my past with grace —not as a burden, but as a testament to my survival. And now, maybe it was time to allow myself a little vulnerability again. To risk. To hope. I had been living so long in the specter of what had been, I had almost forgotten the promise of what could be.

CHAPTER 26

In the days that followed, Andrew and I did our best to maintain a semblance of normalcy. We went about our daily routines, exchanging pleasantries and sharing friendly meals. There was an unspoken agreement to ignore the elephant in the room. Andrew never brought up the incident from that night, nor did I. But there was something different, something more profound in our interactions. The air seemed charged whenever we were in the same room, as if there was an invisible thread tying us together, taunting us with a connection we were too afraid to acknowledge.

As promised, Andrew arranged for Judy and me to see Rosie at the jail. On the drive over, Judy was unusually quiet. She sat rigidly against the seat, her hands clenched tightly in her lap as she watched the world go by. I could see the tension etched in the lines of her face, in the set of her mouth.

"Do you still want to do this?" I asked as I turned the car onto the island.

She didn't respond at first, staring blankly at the building and trees that passed our field of vision. "Yes," she finally said, her voice steady despite the tension tightening every muscle in her body. "I need to know that she's all right."

The jail was a run-down building with peeling paint and rusted old bars. Rosie was sitting on the cold, hard bed when we walked in. Her face lit up slightly as she saw us, a warm smile cutting through the fear in her eyes. Her hair, once lustrous and vibrant, was now dull and tangled, and there was a pallor to her skin that suggested weeks of confinement. But it was the bruised innocence in her eyes that struck me the most.

"How are you holding up?" I asked as I took a seat on the cold stool. "Are they treating you all right?"

She shrugged, her smile feeble. "As well as can be expected," she said, her voice softer than I remembered. "I'm trying to stay hopeful. It's not easy, but I'm trying."

My heart ached for her.

"I can only imagine," said Judy. "It's a mess out there." She gestured vaguely toward the small window. "The town is split right down the middle."

Rosie nodded, her fingers grazing over the cold bars of her cell. "I can hear them sometimes... At night when it's quiet, I can hear them shouting and arguing. It feels like the town is tearing itself apart because of me."

There was an unbearable sadness in her voice that made me want to reach out and comfort her. But I was hesitant, uncertain of what my touch would mean in this place where every action had a consequence.

"It's not your fault, Rosie," said Judy. "Whoever did this to Peter is responsible."

The mention of his name brought tears to Rosie's eyes, reflecting a sorrow that words could hardly express. "Peter." Her fingers curled tighter around the bars, knuckles white from the pressure. "I'm not even sure how to feel about him anymore, given everything I've learned."

"I know," I said. "This isn't fair to you. It's not fair to anyone." I wanted to keep things friendly, but there was a question I'd been dying to ask Rosie ever since I agreed to help

Andrew. "Rosie, they say Peter was cheating on you. Is that true? And if so, did you know about it?"

Her hand slid from the bars, and she looked at me. "Yes, but I didn't do it, Sara. I would never hurt Peter."

I searched her eyes for even an ounce of deceit but found none. "I know. This other woman Peter was seeing... Do you know who she was?"

Rosie hesitated, her gaze dropping to her lap as she traced the faded lines on her chipped nail polish. "I... I have my suspicions," she said finally. "But I've no proof. And honestly, if I tell you and I'm wrong..."

Judy placed her hand gently on Rosie's. "You don't have to say anything more if you're not ready."

I shot Judy a look of impatience, but she returned it with one of understanding and care. I knew how hard this was for her, seeing her friend in such a vulnerable state. But I had a job to do, and no matter how difficult, I had to push forward.

"Judy's right, Rosie," I said. "But we're here to help. If you have any idea who this woman might be, it could be the key to proving your innocence."

Rosie looked back at me, her eyes reflecting her internal struggle. It was the rawest version of her I had ever seen. "There's a woman at Peter's office," she began, her voice shaky. "Her name is Linda. A couple of months ago, they worked on a project together. Not long after, he started coming home late. He said it was because of the workload, but there were nights he didn't come home at all. At first, I thought nothing of it. But then...Peter started changing. He became distant, preoccupied. Whenever I asked him about his work, he'd brush me off. He started wearing cologne, something he never cared for before. It was the little things, Sara, the little changes that tipped me off."

A shiver ran down my spine as I listened to Rosie describe the subtle shifts in Peter's behavior. "And this Linda... Can you tell me more about her... what she looked like, what kind of car she drives?"

Rosie chewed her lower lip, a distant expression in her eyes. "I only saw her once," she explained. "She was petite. I remember because she was so much smaller than Peter. Auburn hair, dark eyes... I don't remember much else about her, but she drove this fancy car. A Cadillac, I think."

Alarm bells went off in my head. "Did you say Cadillac?"

Rosie nodded. "A light blue one with a chrome grille."

"Did you tell the police about this?" Judy asked.

Rosie shook her head. "No. They never asked me. Why?"

I glanced at Judy, then shifted my gaze back to Rosie. "Because that car matches the description of a vehicle seen frequenting Peter's house," I said, a growing sense of unease settling over me.

Rosie paled, looking as though she might be sick. "What do you mean? You think Linda had something to do with Peter's death?"

"I don't know," I said as the pieces started to come together in my head. "But one thing's for sure—I need to find her, and quick."

After telling Andrew what Rosie had shared about Linda, we decided to further our investigation. From my pocket, I pulled out the photograph of Peter's office staff that I had managed to secure earlier from his company's Human Resources department. Among the cheerful faces was a petite woman with auburn hair and dark eyes.

I tapped the photo with my finger, staring at the woman's

image. "This must be her, don't you think?" I asked, showing it to Andrew.

He leaned over to take a closer look, his brow furrowing in thought. "She certainly matches Rosie's description."

"And that of Peter's neighbor. Is there any way we can get her address?"

Andrew made a couple of phone calls and within an hour we had our answer.

"She lives on Highland Drive in Manns Harbor," he said, looking from the address he'd written down to me. "You up for a drive?"

* * *

The journey to Manns Harbor was silent and tense, every passing mile marker bringing us closer to a potentially pivotal confrontation. As we pulled onto Highland Drive, a sense of dread washed over me. As we turned the bend, Andrew slowed the car, and there it was.

The house was modest, standing alone with a shroud of vines creeping up its brick facade. It was the kind of place that could hide secrets, and the light blue Cadillac parked in the driveway seemed to beckon us toward it.

Andrew shot me a glance, his fingers drumming on the steering wheel. "Ready?"

I nodded, pulling at the door handle before I could change my mind.

We approached the house, climbing the steps to the front door with careful, calculated movements. I glanced at Andrew, my heart pounding against my ribcage. He gave a curt nod before knocking on the worn wooden door. For a moment, the only sound was the distant chirping of birds. And then footsteps—soft, hesitant. The door creaked open to reveal a petite woman with auburn hair and dark eyes. Her expression was wary, the creases around her eyes perhaps evidence of worry and sleepless nights.

"Can I help you?"

Andrew introduced us and asked if we could speak with her for a few minutes. Linda hesitated, then stepped aside to let us in. As we crossed the threshold, I took in the simple adornments of the home—faded family photos and an abundance of books. The reality of Linda's life felt far removed from the image I had painted in my mind.

"Please, have a seat." She gestured toward the worn-out couch as she shuffled into the living room.

I exchanged a glance with Andrew. We both sat down, our eyes unconsciously scanning the room. It was a domestic scene that was almost too normal to be noteworthy. The coffee table held a scattering of magazines and a teacup, its contents long cold. A half-finished crossword lay atop a stack of newspapers on the end table.

"Linda, we're here on behalf of Rosalie Flores," said Andrew, his voice cutting through the stillness of the room. "She's the woman accused of killing Peter Sullivan. I believe you knew him, didn't you?"

Her eyes widened, and for a moment, she looked like a frightened deer caught in headlights. "Peter, yes," she stammered. "He and I were...well, we were lovers." She looked away, her hands twisting the hem of her faded blouse.

"We know," Andrew said, his tone soft but firm. "And we believe you might have something to tell us that could help clear Rosalie's name."

Linda's gaze flicked toward us and then away again. "I

don't know what you're talking about."

Andrew leaned forward, his elbows resting on his knees as he studied Linda. "We are not here to accuse or judge you, Linda," he reassured her. "Our only goal is to help Rosalie get a fair trial."

A silent battle waged in her eyes, a tug of war between fear and the flames of some buried truth she'd been holding on to for too long. She clenched her hands into fists, nails digging into her palms as if the pain could somehow distract her from the reality of our presence.

"All right," Linda finally said. "I'll tell you what I know. But I'm not sure how much help I can be."

Over the next few minutes, Linda told us about her relationship with Peter Sullivan, about the late nights they spent together at his house in Nags Head, and their plans for the future.

"We were in love," she said. "I didn't even know about Rosalie until a couple of days before Peter died. I found a letter in the pocket of his coat from her. She was begging him to leave me, to go back to her. I confronted him and we fought. He told me he was going to end things with her, that he loved me and only me." Her voice shook as she recounted the heated exchange, her knuckles white as she wrung her hands together. "And then two days later, he was dead. I woke up to the news that he had been killed, and Rosalie was the prime suspect. I've been here...hiding, ever since."

Andrew leaned back in his seat, crossing his arms over his chest. "Did Peter ever mention being afraid of Rosalie? Or anyone else for that matter?"

Linda shook her head, her hair dancing around her face like a swirl of autumn leaves. "No. Peter wasn't afraid of anyone, certainly not someone like Rosalie, or even me for that matter. The only thing that scared him was losing his wealth. He was constantly paranoid about his financial standing, always checking stocks and making shady deals to keep his money rolling."

"Shady deals?" Andrew raised an eyebrow, seemingly intrigued by this new piece of information.

"Yes. He was involved in some sort of illicit trade. I'm not sure what exactly, but he always had these strange people coming over to the house... Men with cold eyes and briefcases full of cash. Peter told me it was nothing, just business. But after a while, I knew something was amiss."

Andrew sat up, interest flashing in his eyes, a predator catching scent of its prey. "Did you ever meet these men? Do you remember names, faces?"

Linda frowned. "I...I don't know. I mean, there were so many of them, and they all looked kinda alike. But you should probably talk to Graham Walden, he was Peter's business associate. He came by a few times when these men were there... seemed to know them."

Andrew jotted down the name on his notepad. "Graham Walden. Got it. And where would we find this Graham Walden?"

"I don't know. He lives in Charleston, I'm not sure exactly where. But I'd be careful if I were you," Linda warned. "These men, they're...dangerous. They were never violent toward me, but there was something about them, the way they moved. It was like walking among sleeping lions."

"I'll take that under advisement." Andrew stood, signaling the end of the conversation. "Thanks for your time, Linda. I'm going to alert the sheriff about everything you've told me. We'll look into Graham Walden and his associates. In the meantime, keep a low profile, at least until we can get an officer out here to watch your house."

Linda nodded, letting out a sigh that seemed to drain the life from her. "Thank you," she said. "Both of you. You don't know the toll this has taken on me."

"What do you think?" Andrew asked as we made our way back to the car. "Do you think she's telling the truth or lying to us?"

I recalled Linda's words, that look of genuine fear in her eyes. "I think she's being truthful. Which means this is much bigger than a simple small town love triangle."

"Agreed," said Andrew, opening the door for me. "If Peter was involved in some shady dealings, his murder could have been a hit. And if that's the case, we all need to watch our backs."

CHAPTER 27

With the authorities now investigating Peter's business dealings, Andrew and I were free to focus on the facts of the case and how we might tie them together to paint a picture of Rosie's innocence.

As the trial progressed, so did my fascination with it. I expressed my interest to Andrew over dinner one night, telling him how I wished I had chosen law as my path of study in school rather than mathematics.

"It's never too late," he said, smiling warmly over his glass of red wine. "With the proper tutelage, you could be ready to take the bar in just a couple of years."

"I don't know," I said, allowing my mind to wander toward possibilities I had never before entertained. "Do you really think I have what it takes to do what you do?"

Andrew studied me, his eyes sparkling with genuine interest. For a moment, he seemed lost in thought, then he smiled again. "I have seen the determination in you, the tenacity. The way you have supported Rosie through all of this, it shows character. Law isn't just about knowing rules and regulations. It's about a sense of justice, the ability to empathize, and the willingness to stand up for what is right even if the whole world is against you."

His words stirred up something within me. I had never seen myself through the lens he was providing, and it was both surprising and exciting. The idea of becoming a lawyer—not just any lawyer, but one like Andrew, always calm amidst the storm, standing up for what was right regardless of the odds— began to take root.

After that, the stars seemed to align. Andrew and I were drawn to each other, our connection deepening with each passing day. When Andrew wasn't trying Rosie's case, we would sit for hours, talking about our hopes and dreams. With each shared secret we felt the pieces of our broken hearts slowly starting to mend. Eventually, I let go of the pain from my past, choosing instead to focus on this newfound hope blossoming within me.

Even Judy began to notice the change in me. She watched with curious eyes as I hummed while preparing meals or twirled around the room, caught up in my own happiness. She, too, had grown quite fond of Andrew, his quiet demeanor and unwavering dedication slowly winning her over. One morning, while preparing breakfast, Judy asked if Andrew was going to become a permanent fixture in our lives. It was a question I had also begun to ponder.

"I don't know," I said as I kneaded dough for the morning biscuits. "I mean, he's a great guy and all, but..."

"But what?"

"I don't know. I just... I feel guilty, that's all."

"For what?"

"For being happy, I guess," I admitted, my hands momentarily stilling in the dough. "After everything that's happened to Rosie, it just seems wrong to feel so joyful."

She looked at me and tilted her head a bit, studying me with those piercing blue eyes of hers. "You know that's not how Rosie would want you to feel, right? You can't put your happiness on hold just because she's going through a tough time. We all have our battles to fight, and you deserve to be happy. Besides, Rosie's going to be fine. She's a fighter, and I have faith that Andrew will find a way to clear her name. Then, things can go back to normal around here."

Part of me was hopeful that Andrew would be able to clear her name. But another part of me feared what would happen when the trial was over.

"I just don't want to get ahead of myself. I like Andrew a lot, but I don't see how this can work. I mean, he's only here until the trial ends, then it's back to Atlanta for him. Meanwhile, I'll still be here, stuck in this small town, serving cold pie and coffee to tourists and sailors."

"Easy," Judy said, seeming to take offense to my comment.

"Sorry, I didn't mean it like that. It's just... I've been down this road before, and I don't want to give my heart away only to have it smashed into pieces again."

Judy didn't say anything for a long time, studying me with those wise eyes of hers. Then she sighed, draping an arm over my shoulder. "I hate to break it to you, doll, but love is always a risk. You can't let the fear of getting hurt stop you from the joy it brings. You're right, Andrew might leave, and he might break your heart, but what if he doesn't? What if he's the one? You'll never know unless you take that leap."

I thought about her words for a long time that night as I lay in bed, staring at the ceiling. The silvery moonlight streamed through the window, casting eerie shadows across the room. I thought about Andrew's smile, the way his eyes crinkled when he laughed. I remembered the warmth of his hand on mine, and how it felt as though electricity was coursing through my veins. I remembered the softness of his voice, a soothing melody that lulled my fears and insecurities. And I remembered the profound longing that gnawed at my heart when he was not around, a longing that no amount of denial could silence.

Outside, a gentle breeze blew in from the ocean, its cool touch bringing some comfort to my troubled mind. Maybe Judy was right. What if he was the one? What if by denying myself the prospect of love, I was denying myself a chance at happiness? My heart fluttered at the thought, a delicate bird yearning to take flight. I had always tried to be practical, to put reason above emotion. But love wasn't about practicality. It was about taking risks, diving headfirst into the unknown. And although every fiber of my being was telling me to resist, to protect my heart, I knew in the deepest part of my soul that it was a battle I was losing. The tide of my emotions was too strong.

So, I decided right then and there, that I wouldn't hold back anymore. I would stop trying to predict the future, stop trying to shield my heart from potential pain. Instead, I would let myself feel, let myself fall, and let myself love.

After dinner the next night, Andrew and I took a walk on the beach, letting the breeze rustle our hair and the sand slip through our toes. The stars overhead shone brightly, illuminating the darkness that surrounded us. I could hear the ebb and flow of the waves, a comforting lullaby that filled the silence between us.

"Andrew, there's something I need to tell you...before this goes any further."

He stopped and turned to look at me, his expression inquisitive yet calm. The gentle moonlight highlighted the contours of his face, making his eyes shimmer with an intensity that took my breath away. "Yes?"

I laid out for him the entire sordid tale, from my plot to

spoil Jack's proposal to the night he told me to leave, sparing no detail. When I was done, I was in tears, consumed by the pain and guilt that had plagued me for so long.

"It's all right," Andrew whispered, drawing me close as sobs wracked my body, his fingers gently tracing circles on my back. I clung to him tightly, seeking solace in his presence.

"I loved him," I whispered between sobs. "I thought ruining his proposal would make him see that he should be with me. But instead, I lost him forever."

Andrew held me tighter, his embrace a shield against the remorse that echoed through my words. Neither of us spoke for a long time, the only sounds the whispers of the ocean and my intermittent sobs.

"I hope you don't think less of me," I said after composing myself.

"Never." He pulled back a little, gently lifting my chin so I would look at him. His eyes were warm and kind as they met mine. "We all do foolish things for love, me included. As long as we're confessing secrets, I have one of my own."

We found a piece of driftwood and sat at the water's edge, letting the waves lap at our feet. "Go on," I urged him gently.

His eyes turned distant, as if he was gazing far into the past. "I was married once," he revealed. "Her name was Gail. We were young...foolishly in love. We thought we could conquer the world together, that nothing could tear us apart. But we were wrong, and life had other plans." He paused, took a deep breath and continued. "She fell out of love with me and into the arms of another man. She left without a word, without an explanation, just a note on the kitchen table. I had built my entire world around her. To have it all crumble, to find out that my love wasn't enough...it broke me." His voice hitched and he looked away. "Like you, I thought I could win her back, that if I fought hard enough, she would see that our love was worth fighting for. So I chased her. I sent letters, flowers, tried to talk to her whenever I could. But every attempt was met with coldness, indifference. It was as if the woman I had married, the woman who had promised to love and cherish me, had vanished. It took me years to accept that she was gone, that our love story was over."

I sat there, stunned at his confession. Andrew, the always strong, indestructible man I had come to know, had been heartbroken. His pain matched mine and suddenly, I felt less alone.

"I'm sorry," I said, taking his hand in mine.

He gave a half-hearted smile, his gaze still focused on the inky horizon. "Don't be. It was a long time ago." His eyes met mine and I saw the flicker of pain behind them. "Besides, everything happens for a reason. If Gail hadn't broken my heart all those years ago, I wouldn't have been able to understand your pain now. I wouldn't have been able to be here with you, in this moment."

His confession hung in the air between us, a bridge of shared heartbreak that felt healing instead of painful. If there was any doubt before, now there was none. I was hopelessly in love with Andrew.

Unwilling to let the moment pass, I leaned forward, closing the gap between us, and softly brushed my lips against his. He stiffened in surprise before melting into the kiss. His arm moved to encircle my waist, pulling me closer to him.

His lips were warm, a balm to my fractured heart. The world seemed to fall away, the heartbreak and pain of the past melting into the night. It was just Andrew and me, two broken souls finding solace in each other under the silent watch of the stars.

His hand gently roved to the small of my back, holding me to him as if I were the most precious treasure he had ever held. The kiss deepened, and I felt a fluttering in my stomach, a sensation that was both terrifying and exhilarating. He tasted like the wine we had shared earlier, sweet with a hint of something dark and mysterious. I drank in his essence, each kiss more intoxicating than the last.

We pulled apart, breathless, our foreheads resting against each other. A soft smile played on his lips, reaching his weary eyes, giving them that sparkle I had come to love. His thumb gently traced circles on my cheek, his touch soft and tender.

"It's funny," he said over the whispering wind. "I didn't think I could ever feel like this again."

"Neither did I." I traced the outline of his face with my fingers, trying to commit every detail to memory.

His hand slipped from my back and reached for the zipper on my dress. His touch was slow and delicate, every movement respectful and patient. His eyes were fixed on mine, asking for consent that I was more than willing to give. The dress slid down my shoulders, landing softly at my feet. He took a moment to study me, his eyes filled with admiration and desire.

I watched as his gaze traveled down my body, and then back up to meet my eyes. The intensity in his look caused a soft blush to creep up my cheeks. His gentle touch ignited a fire within me, a fire that had been dormant for so long.

He removed his clothes and slowly wrapped his arms around me, pulling me closer until there was not an inch of space between us. His hands cradled my bare shoulders, his fingers tracing patterns against my skin as if he was trying to engrave his touch into my very being. He looked at me with such tenderness, such raw emotion, that it made my heart swell.

The stars above us twinkled in approval, casting us in a gentle glow as we drew even closer. Andrew's hands shifted to my waist, his touch sending shivers of anticipation down my spine. His lips found mine again, this time with a hunger that matched the fire burning within me.

As our bodies entwined under the blanket of the night, there was no world beyond us. Everything faded into insignificance. His hands moved, strong and sure, tracing the contours of my body as if he was exploring uncharted territory. Andrew's lips traveled from my mouth to the curve of my neck and down to my collarbone, showering me with kisses that left a trail of fire in their wake.

His gentle touch was replaced by a sense of urgency. His fingers danced across the small of my back, delicately tracing the curve of my spine. His lips then found mine again, and he kissed me with a fervor that left me breathless. His hands roamed freely, each touch further affirming his need for me.

Andrew moved, pulling me down onto my dress.

The rough texture beneath my bare skin was a stark contrast to the warmth of his body pressed against mine. He hovered above me, his striking silhouette framed by the luminous silver of the moon. His gaze was intense, his eyes flickering with an emotion that sent my heart racing.

His hands slid to my sides, his fingers trailing a tantalizing path up my waist, over my ribcage, and coming to rest on my breasts. His touch was impossibly light, yet every nerve seemed to burn where his skin met mine.

He leaned down, his lips brushing against my earlobe. "I love you, Sara."

"I love you, too," I breathed, reaching my hands up to tangle in his hair, pulling him closer.

A soft sigh escaped his lips as he gently lowered himself onto me, our bodies fitting together as though they were made for one another.

His mouth found mine again in a kiss that was a symphony of passion and tenderness. I tasted the salt of the sea on his lips, savored the warmth of his breath mingling with mine. I reveled in the intoxicating scent of him, all woodsy and earthy and masculine.

Slowly, agonizingly slowly, Andrew began to move. Each motion was measured and deliberate, more an act of love than lust. Every nerve in my body seemed to come alive under his touch, sparking with an intensity that left me gasping for breath.

We moved together in a rhythm as ancient as the stars, two hearts beating in sync, two spirits melding into one. The world beyond our intimate cocoon ceased to exist. We were adrift, suspended in a timeless space where only we existed.

Our shared pleasure echoed in the silent night, our bodies curved and tangled in a dance that was both primal and exquisite. His breath hitched as he pressed his forehead against mine, his eyes locking onto mine with an intensity that rendered me breathless. He was everywhere—his scent, his touch, his taste—completely enveloping me until I didn't know where I ended and he began.

Time seemed to stretch and warp around us. Minutes bled into hours, reality fading into a distant memory. There was only Andrew and me, our bodies entwined, bare and vulnerable beneath the twinkling canopy of stars. Every whispered word, every shared breath, every stroke of skin against skin drew us closer together.

His fingers gently caressed my face as he looked down at me, his eyes sparkling, as if the world was brighter because I was there. I reached up to trace the contours of his face—the rugged jawline, the stubble-covered cheeks, the perfectly shaped lips— all pieces that made him who he was.

Our heartbeats slowed down as the night grew colder around us, but the heat between us remained. My fingers danced on his chest, and I could feel the steady beating of his heart, a rhythm that was now as familiar to me as my own.

That night on the beach, Andrew became more than just my lover. He was my confidant, my anchor in the stormy sea of my past.

CHAPTER 28

Each day after was a discovery, an exploration of two souls who had been yearning for meaningful connection. As the trial entered its third week, our relationship deepened even more. I saw in Andrew a true partner, someone who understood that life was not always fair, but that together, we could navigate its treacherous waters. And in me, Andrew found a sanctuary, a home he'd been unconsciously seeking.

Even as the courtroom walls echoed with damning testimonies and piercing cross-examinations, we found peace in our shared lunches. We spoke not of the trial, but of dreams, aspirations, and the little things that form one's essence. In those fleeting moments, it felt as though we had created a world within a world, suspended in time, immune to the chaos unfolding outside. There was a certain solace we found in each other's company that diminished the gravity of the trial, making it feel more like an unwelcome guest than the all-encompassing threat it was.

"Do you think the sheriff will uncover any evidence in time to help Rosie?" I asked Andrew one afternoon as we sat in the park, eating our lunch.

"Honestly, I don't know." He took a bite of his sandwich, watching a group of children playing by the pond. The golden rays of the sun kissed the ripple on the water, creating an intricate pattern of shimmering gold and azure. It was then I saw a flicker of something unrecognizable in Andrew's eyes. An elusive shadow, gone before I could fully comprehend it.

"What are you thinking about?" I asked.

Andrew was silent for a moment. He seemed to be collecting his thoughts, trying to form them into words. The absence of his usual quick responses added weight to my unease.

"Do you ever wonder if Rosie actually did it? If she's the one who killed Peter?"

"No, of course not," I answered reflexively. "Tell me you're not starting to have doubts."

"No." He shook his head. "It's just... I'm trying to look at this through the eyes of the jury...see what they see, instead of what we know."

"I suppose that's fair," I said. "What is it you think they see?"

"I think they see a lot of uncertainty, a lot of confusion. They see a young woman who they don't want to believe committed this crime, but at the same time understand that the evidence against her is compelling."

My heart ached at his words. I believed in Rosie's innocence with all my heart, but the evidence...

"As much as it pains me to say it, if I were on that jury, removed from my personal relationship with Rosie, and without evidence to the contrary, I'd be leaning toward the very conviction we're trying so desperately to prevent."

Andrew didn't say anything for a long time, his eyes fixed on the children by the pond. Finally, he turned back to me, his face grave. "I know it looks bad, but we must never lose faith. Rosie is innocent, and we have to trust that the truth will come out, one way or another."

Despite the need for urgency, it felt as if Sheriff Callahan and his team were moving at a snail's pace. Their methodical, almost lethargic approach was infuriating to watch. They were checking into Peter's business dealings, of course, but I was certain they were treating her as guilty until proven innocent.

As another week drew to a close, our frustrations mounted. Rosie's trial was inching closer to the finish line, yet there were still no breakthroughs, no miracles to prove her innocence. The atmosphere around us became tense, hope slowly dwindling with each passing day.

We felt the weight of the world on our shoulders as we sat in Andrew's makeshift office, poring over the case files that seemed to multiply each day.

"How much longer do you think the trial will last?" I asked as I rubbed my tired eyes.

"Another week, maybe longer," said Andrew.

For the first time since we met, I felt a twinge of fear. What would happen when the trial ended? Would he leave Kitty Hawk and return to his life in Atlanta, leaving me behind? Or would it somehow be possible for us to build a life together, whether it be here, there, or somewhere new? "And then what?"

He looked up at me, his eyes softening as they met mine. "And then we wait for the verdict."

"I know. I mean, after that?"

"I'm not sure what you mean."

"With us," I said. "What will become of us?"

That appeared to be a tougher question to answer. Eventually, Andrew set down the manila folder he was reading and gave me his full attention. "I don't know. To be honest, I've grown quite fond of this place...and of you."

His words echoed in the silent evening, settling into the crevices of my heart. I looked at him, at the sincerity in his eyes, and felt an unfamiliar warmth seep through me. I wanted to believe that we had a future together, that he would stay and we could build a life in this little coastal town. But I was also aware that fate could be cruel, and I didn't want to set myself up for another heartbreak.

Andrew seemed to sense my thoughts. He reached across the table and squeezed my hand gently, reassuring me without words.

"But I'm also aware of the life I left, the life that's waiting for me in Atlanta."

"What if you didn't go back? What if you stayed here instead? You said yourself this place has grown on you."

He sighed, a long, drawn-out exhale that seemed to carry with it the weight of the world. "I wish it were that simple, Sara. I truly do. But there are obligations I can't ignore. My practice is there, my family."

"I understand," I said, though I didn't really. I had left home once, had shrugged off the shackles of my own obligations to pursue a life of independence here in Kitty Hawk. But Andrew was not me. His ties were stronger, his roots ran deeper.

"Could you ever consider coming with me?"

Andrew's voice broke through my tangled thoughts.

"Come with you? To Atlanta?"

He nodded. "Yes. It would be different, I know. But perhaps it could be a good different, a new adventure...for us both."

The idea was terrifying. I had found a home in this small town by the ocean, had built a life away from Tennessee and the dozens of broken dreams. Yet the thought of losing Andrew was equally unbearable.

"I..." The words stuck in my throat as I wrestled with the ramifications of his proposal. I glanced down at his hand on mine, the warmth of his touch seeping into me. Was he really offering a life together or was this just a desperate plea, born out of our fear of an inevitable goodbye? "I need to think about it," I finally said, taking back my hand.

There was a look in his eyes, a mix of disappointment and understanding, but he remained silent, respecting my need for space.

* * *

Needing to clear my head, I went for a drive. Unknowingly, I found myself heading toward Manteo, retracing the same route Rosie had taken the night of Peter's death. The empty road stretched before me in the moonlight, the salty sea breeze filling the car. My thoughts were consumed by Andrew and his proposal. The night Peter died, Rosie had been fleeing from her own heartbreak, running from a man who had betrayed her. Now I was on the same road, torn between my heart and home, fleeing from the fear of a potential heartbreak.

When I arrived in Manteo, I parked near the theater, the lights from the marquee clearly visible through the windshield, and I remembered the last time Rosie, Judy, and I were there. We had gone to watch a matinee showing of *A Streetcar Named Desire*, giggling like schoolgirls as we shared popcorn from a single bucket. We sat in the front row, Rosie clutching my hand tightly during the intense scenes, her eyes wide with fear and anticipation. Judy, on the other hand, had been engrossed, her eyes never leaving the screen.

That seemed so long ago, back when our lives were simpler. The memory stirred a deep longing within me, a yearning for that sense of security and peace. Yet, I knew those days were locked in the past. Our lives had changed irrevocably since then. As much as I hated to admit it, if Andrew and I couldn't clear Rosie's name, our lives would never be the same again.

I sat quietly, going over the details of the case in my head. There was so much that didn't add up—the discrepancies between Peter's reported time of death and the time Rosie was seen leaving the theater, the shaky motive, and the bloodstained shirt, placed conspicuously in Rosie's laundry.

I reached into the glove compartment and pulled out the police report that Andrew had given me. With the glow of the theater marquee lights illuminating the car, I began to skim through the notes once again.

My eyes traced the familiar lines of the narrative, each word as familiar as the lines from my favorite book. But this time, as I read through the report, something caught my eye. A minor detail, almost insignificant, that the authorities seemed to have overlooked in their initial investigation. The report mentioned a road closure on Roanoke Island that night due to flooding. Curiously, it was the road Rosie would have taken to get home from the theater.

A glimmer of hope flickered in my heart as I quickly pulled out the worn map that was crumpled in the side pocket of the passenger seat. I traced Rosie's possible routes home that night, finding only one that would have gotten her off the island.

It was almost midnight when I knocked on Andrew's motel room door. He answered, hair tousled and eyes blinking sleepily in the harsh light that spilled from the parking lot. I held out the police report and the map, the initial panic having settled into a steady determination.

"I think I found something," I muttered, brushing past him into the room. The bed was unmade, clothes thrown haphazardly across the room. His briefcase was still open, case files scattered around it. The room smelled of stale coffee and leftovers. "I think we've been looking at this all wrong." I unfolded the map on the unoccupied part of the bed, pointing to Roanoke Island. "According to the police report, Betty Arnwine reported seeing Rosie leave the theater at precisely 9:10."

Andrew nodded along.

"And the medical examiner has the time of death at 9:30, right?"

"Thereabouts."

I stared at the map, calculating again the distance and time it would have taken Rosie to get from the theater to her home. "She didn't do it," I said, looking up at Andrew. "It's impossible."

Andrew got up and took a closer look. "How do you figure?"

"It's simple, don't you see?"

"Simple to you, perhaps."

"It's a little over twenty miles from Manteo to Rosie's house, right?"

"Yeah, so? That gives her just enough time. I drove it myself, remember?"

"Yes, but you did it in the daylight, and on a dry day with no traffic. That night, there was an awful storm. The roads were treacherous, and power was out to half of Roanoke Island. The rain was pouring so hard that there were reports of flooding all along the sound. It's right there in the police report." He took another look while I continued. "If Peter was killed when they say he was, Rosie would've had roughly twenty minutes to make the drive and commit the crime. Which means she would have to be going over sixty miles an hour, non-stop."

"Okay, so maybe she drove really fast," said Andrew, playing devil's advocate.

"Maybe, but the road she would normally have taken off

the island was shut down due to flooding, which means the detour she took would have added at least another half-hour to her trip. Plus, visibility was poor, and the roads were slick. It's not just improbable. It's impossible."

Andrew considered the evidence, the wheels clearly turning in his head. "This detour...is it anywhere in the police report?"

"Yes," I said. "It's all there, in black and white."

"Holy shit! If you're right...then the timeline...it's all wrong."

"Exactly," I pointed out, my finger tracing the path she would have taken to get from Manteo to Kitty Hawk. "No way Rosie could have killed Peter when they say she did."

Andrew stood silent for a moment, processing the flurry of information. His gaze shifted from the map to the police report and back again before he finally slumped into his chair. He ran a hand through his hair, looking both frustrated and relieved. "Do you know what this means?"

"It means Rosie is innocent," I said, trying to keep the satisfaction out of my voice.

"Not only that, but it also means we still have a killer on the loose," Andrew said gravely. "And an innocent woman being held for a crime she didn't commit."

"So, what do we do next?"

"We take this evidence to the judge, first thing tomorrow morning."

"And what about the real killer?" I asked, a trace of worry creeping into my voice. "Don't we have to find who did this?"

"We've done our part," he said, a look of determination hardening in his eyes. "Now, it's up to the sheriff to bring the real killer to justice."

Present

"Yes!" Diane shouted, throwing her hands into the air. "I knew she didn't do it."

I laughed, remembering the same exuberance I'd felt when I had first put the pieces together. "And that's the moment I knew I wanted to be a lawyer."

Diane smiled, her eyes shining with admiration and curiosity. "Wow! So that's how it all started?"

"Yes. It was a wild ride, but it showed me the power of truth and justice. Rosie's case wasn't simple, but it set me on a path I would never have found otherwise."

Judy appeared then, letting us know supper was ready.

Diane glanced at her watch, then back at me, a look of disappointment on her face. "Do we really have to stop? I was hoping to find out if they ever caught the real killer."

I got up and patted her gently on the shoulder. "Don't worry, dear. There's still plenty of this story left to tell."

CHAPTER 29

Friday

With only two days left in Diane's visit, we decided to start early. Instead of eating in the kitchen or on the veranda, we settled into our familiar places in the library, letting Judy serve us breakfast there. After we'd both had a few bites of omelet and sipped our coffee, Diane switched on the tape recorder.

"Tell me," she began, "how did it feel knowing you had cracked the case?"

I leaned back in my chair, the soft leather yielding beneath me. "Well," I said, drawing a deep breath, "it was a mix of relief and validation, I suppose. But it was short-lived, because I knew my job wasn't done until Rosie was found innocent and released from jail."

Kitty Hawk, NC

July 1963

I hardly slept that night, my insomnia fueled by thoughts of what would take place later that morning. Andrew was prepared to drop a bombshell in court, one that would inevitably alter the course of the trial, but also shake the very foundation of our small town.

When dawn finally broke, I stood in front of the bathroom mirror, staring at my reflection, trying to muster up the courage to face what was coming. The bags under my eyes were more pronounced, the lines on my face deeper from the sleepless night. I looked like a woman burdened by an enormous secret, and that was precisely what it was.

After a glass of water and a hastily eaten piece of toast, I put on my best suit, the one usually reserved for Sundays, but today demanded something more formal. I tidied up my hair, put on a small amount of lipstick—not too flashy—and took one last look in the mirror. The woman staring back at me had a certain resolve in her eyes. I reflected on the journey that had led me here. I thought about Jack and Ellie, and those early days when I'd first arrived in Kitty Hawk. I thought about all the times I'd wanted to go back, to tell Jack I was sorry for lying to him, to try and see if there was still hope for us. But that felt so long ago now, and so futile. Jack had moved on and so had I, in our own ways. More than that, I was happy now, in a way I had never been happy before, and that was something I wouldn't trade for anything.

Turning back, I picked up my purse and glanced at the picture on the nightstand, the one of Judy, Rosie, and me taken outside the restaurant. And I thought back several weeks, before all this began. I thought about how innocent we were then, blissfully unaware of the turmoil that was about to engulf us. I also thought about those early days, after Rosie was arrested, and how quickly the townspeople had taken sides. The old courthouse on Marshall Collins Drive had become a symbol of the deep divide. It was as though an invisible line had been drawn down the center of town, severing friendships and even families. Most of the men had sided with the prosecution, while the women, many having known Rosie for years, remained staunch believers in her innocence.

Even the restaurant wasn't immune to the division. It had become a battlefield of opinions as people gathered for meals. Conversations were tense, often erupting into heated debates. As much as I tried to remain neutral, I couldn't. My relationships with Rosie and Andrew placed me squarely in the crossfire, causing me to face uncomfortable questions and hostile glares.

But none of that seemed to matter now. I knew today was about much more than heated debates and fractured friendships. Today was the day when an innocent woman would be set free.

I left the pier and headed toward the courthouse, arriving earlier than normal. I wanted to be there before Andrew, to have a few moments to calm my nerves and center my thoughts before the storm hit.

Once inside, I watched as the seats began to fill with curious onlookers, many of the same faces I'd seen for weeks. Their eyes followed me, their whispers floated through the air as I took my usual spot. Normally, their spearing gazes would have made me uncomfortable, but not today. Today, I knew something they didn't, and that knowledge gave me a sense of power I'd never before experienced.

When court resumed, I sat nervously in the front row, clenching and unclenching the fabric of my skirt. I had never been more nervous in my life.

Rosie entered with the same ghostly pallor she'd carried since the trial began, her eyes scanned the crowd until they landed on me. Her lips pulled into a weak smile before she was directed to her seat. I wanted to return that smile, to signal to her that we had cracked the case, but Andrew had sworn me to secrecy. Instead, I simply nodded in her direction, hoping the warmth in my gaze would convey my reassurance.

I anxiously watched the clock, counting the seconds as they ticked by. The prosecutor and Andrew were nowhere to be seen. Andrew had always been punctual, especially on important occasions—and none was more important than this. The seconds turned into minutes, each one feeling like an eternity. Whispers started to fill the courtroom again, louder this time, questioning their absence. Just as the clock struck 9:15, the heavy double doors at the back of the courtroom swung open. A hush swiftly descended over the room as everyone turned their heads toward the entrance.

It was Andrew who entered first, the look on his face stoic, unreadable. I tried to make eye contact with him, but his gaze did not waver from the path ahead. The prosecutor followed close behind, his face gaunt and pallid, as if he had seen a ghost. He looked around the room nervously, his eyes darting from face to face, before finally landing on me. He offered a slight nod in my direction, but his eyes held a message that was hard to decipher.

The judge was the last to enter, taking his seat behind the bench. With the bang of his gavel, he brought everyone's attention back to the front. His face was stern, as always, but there was something else, something I couldn't put my finger on. His eyes moved over the crowd, pausing slightly as they met mine. The corners of his mouth twitched upward in what could be interpreted as a faint smile. It was unusual, unsettling even.

The courtroom bristled with anticipation as the judge cleared his throat, shuffling through some papers on his desk. My heart pounded in my chest, each beat echoing my mounting anxiety. The judge looked up, his eyes meeting mine for a brief moment before he announced in a voice louder than before, "Ladies and gentlemen, I apologize for my tardiness this morning. I've just come from a rather enlightening discussion with both the prosecution and the defense. I am sure you all understand that in a case of this magnitude, new details can often surface and alter the course of the proceedings significantly."

His eyes were shrouded in an enigmatic veil as he paused for effect. I could almost hear the collective heartbeat of everyone present. The whispers had subsided, replaced by bated breaths and wide, anxious eyes.

Andrew now looked at me, his gaze steady but revealing nothing. His poker face was impressive; years of being in and out of the courtroom had taught him that much. The prosecutor held the same expression, his eyes locked on the judge.

"After discussing with both parties and considering the new evidence that has been brought to light, it has been decided that further investigation is needed to determine the true culprit in this crime," the judge announced.

A chorus of gasps followed his words, rippling through the space like a gust of wind.

I felt the knot in my stomach unclench, just a little as the judge's gavel hit the bench with a resounding crack.

"In the meantime, the defendant is absolved of all charges and is to be released from custody immediately."

I couldn't tell if it was the relief, shock, or pure unadulterated joy that sent Rosie's knees buckling beneath her as the judge's words echoed through the room. Andrew and I rushed to support her as the courtroom erupted into a cacophony of gasps and murmurs, the observers swaying like reeds in a storm. Press, penned in the back, began to scramble, radios crackling and flashbulbs popping. The judge banged his gavel, trying to restore order, but it was like trying to quiet a flock of starlings.

Now that it was all over, Rosalie looked at us with tears in her eyes, a tentative smile playing on her lips. "I can't thank you enough. Both of you," she said, her voice trembling with emotion.

We clapped her on the back, whispering words of encouragement, relief flooding our systems. It was over. Rosalie was free.

The sun outside had never seemed brighter nor the air sweeter as we stepped out of the courthouse. Cameras flashed in our faces and microphones were shoved toward us, but none of it mattered. The world was a haze of joyous disbelief. Ignoring the calls of the reporters, we rushed to a waiting car, leaving the chaos behind.

Present

When I finished telling the story, I looked at Diane, her eyes filled with tears.

"What an amazing story," she said, wiping her cheeks with the back of her hand. "That must have been quite a harrowing experience, for all of you."

"Yes, it was. But I think we all learned something from it. Like faith and perseverance can pay off, even in the face of seemingly insurmountable odds. We learned that truth will always find a way to shine through the darkest shadows. And most importantly, we learned about the resilience of the human spirit, and how it can rise from the ashes, stronger and brighter."

"Indeed," Diane replied, scribbling down my words. "And how is Rosalie doing now?"

I peered out the window for a moment, gathering my thoughts. "Rosie... she's..." I struggled to find the words that could capture the depth of my emotions. "She's no longer with us," I finally said, turning my gaze back to her.

Diane's hand, which was poised to continue writing, froze on the paper. Her eyes held the shock that I had felt when I first heard the news. "I'm sorry, I didn't know," she said, laying down her pen and looking at me with genuine sympathy.

"It's all right," I reassured her, a small and sad smile pulling at the corners of my mouth. "It happened a long time ago."

Diane's eyes softened further. "I'm so sorry for your loss."

"Thank you," I said, appreciating her kind words. But Diane had no idea of just how deep that loss had cut me. Rosie had been more than a friend to me. She was like the sister I never had. She was like family. "I think about her every day," I continued, lost in my own thoughts. "About the first time we met, about the trial, about what happened after..."

CHAPTER 30

Kitty Hawk, NC

July 1963

When the celebration ended, Andrew and I took a short drive down the coast to a place that had become as important to me as my own heartbeat. It was a place where the sea met the sky, a place I had discovered during those first few days when I was new to town, lost and alone.

The Bodie Island lighthouse stood tall against the twilight sky, a beacon of light amidst the encroaching darkness. The air was thick with the scent of salt and seaweed, the crashing of the waves a soothing lullaby. We sat on the hood of the car, huddled together for warmth as we watched the distant lightning play across the tempestuous horizon. There was a promise of a storm in the salt-laden wind, one that echoed the turmoil brewing beneath the calmness of our collected façade.

"I can see why you like it here so much," said Andrew. His voice was soft, almost swallowed by the rolling waves and distant thunder.

"Solitude within chaos," I replied, my gaze fixed on the lighthouse's hypnotic pulse. "It serves as a reminder."

"A reminder?"

"That even in the darkest of times, there's always a beacon

to guide us home."

Andrew remained silent, and I was too afraid to look at him. But I could feel his gaze on me, intense and penetrating. I wanted to kiss him right there, to close the distance that had grown between us since that night. But fear held me back, rooted me in place as the wind howled around us and the sea churned furiously beneath the ominous sky.

"You performed admirably these past few weeks," he said as the first drops of rain fell from the sky. "Taking on a new role, stepping into a world you knew nothing about. You should be proud of yourself. I know I am."

"Thank you," I said, leaning into the warmth of his body.

Andrew offered me a gentle smile. "I mean it," Andrew insisted, looking over at me. "Without you, I couldn't have done this."

His admission lingered in the space between us, vulnerable as the first light of dawn. It was a confession of sorts, an intimate revelation that tipped the scales, pushing me over the edge I'd been teetering on. "I couldn't have done it without you either, Andrew."

As if on cue, the wind picked up, wrapping us in a cocoon of swirling mist. Suddenly, Andrew reached out and took my hand, his fingers interlocking with mine. "You know, Sara, I think you should really consider staying on with me full-time."

"Andrew..."

"No, hear me out," he said. "You've proven yourself more than worthy of the position. Plus, you have the passion, the determination, the empathy. You have everything it takes to make a great lawyer."

"Andrew, I-I don't know," I stammered, shaking my head in disbelief. "I can't just become a lawyer. I mean, sure, I managed not to embarrass myself as your assistant. But a lawyer? I still don't know the first thing about...about..."

"About the law?" Andrew finished for me. "That's what law school is for, Sara. And we have a great one in Georgia."

"But Andrew," I started to protest, but he cut me off.

"Remember the first day we met?" He stared off toward the lighthouse, his gaze lost in the pulsing light. "I saw in you a spark of potential that not many people have. You have a knack for seeking the truth, a quality that's rare and essential in this field. Besides that, you have the courage to stand up for what you believe in, no matter how unpopular or challenging it may seem. And you've got a backbone."

I stared at Andrew, my amusement fading away as I digested his words. My eyes wandered back to the churning sea, to the lighthouse beam sweeping over it like a grand conductor. "Could I really do it?" I murmured, more to myself than to him. "Defend someone's life in the face of overwhelming odds?"

"More than that," Andrew said. "You could change the world. One case at a time."

A bolt of lightning split the night sky, and something inside me shifted. In the sudden illumination, I saw the truth in Andrew's eyes. We were two lost ships, adrift in the vast expanse of life's tumultuous ocean, with only the pulsating lighthouse as our sentinel. Lost, yes, but perhaps not so alone.

With the thunder rumbling around us, our lips met, and in that instant, our souls blended. I was unsure of where he ended, and I began. The kiss was an aching confession of love, a silent echo of our hearts. I knew then that our paths were irrevocably intertwined, that we were destined to weather the storm together.

The deluge that had been teasing at the edges of the horizon pounced, drenching us in a torrent of rain. We didn't move. The water plastered our hair to our skulls, soaked through our clothes and pooled in our laps, but we stayed put, staring at each other with an intensity that put the brooding storm to shame.

"Promise me something," Andrew shouted over the storm. "Promise me that you'll be mine forever."

"Forever is a long time," I said, my voice trembling. "What if I change, or you change? What if..."

"Marry me, Sara," he interrupted. "Marry me, and let's navigate this life together."

"Are you crazy?" I shouted back, half laughing, half crying, the water streaming down my face disguising my tears. "You don't even have a ring."

Andrew jumped off the car, searching the ground for something, anything. He picked up the remnants of a seashell, broken and battered by the relentless waves, a hole having been punched through its center. "This," he said, holding up the seashell. "This will be our ring. Broken, yet beautiful, worn by time and the tide, but surviving. Just like us."

The wind howled in response, as if approving.

He slid back onto the car and took my hand, which was shaking just as much as his was. He threaded the seashell onto my finger, its cold roughness pressing into my skin. "Sara, will you marry me?"

I stared at him, barely able to make out his face through the curtain of rain. My gaze shifted to the makeshift ring on my finger, the shell, scarred and imperfect. I thought of all I had been through, all the hope, the pain, the loss, and the love. I thought then of Andrew and how he had rescued me from the abyss I had found myself in, about how he made me believe in love again, in the endless hope of a future...a future with him.

"And you promise to be with me, through every storm?"

His eyes were resolute, the storm clouds reflecting in his deep blues. "Every single one, no matter how fierce."

An explosion of thunder drowned out my next words, but they were more for myself than him. "You're insane... We're both insane." But then again, maybe only the insane dare to love so deeply, so fearlessly. So, I swallowed my fears, took a deep breath, and gazed into Andrew's earnest eyes. "Yes, Andrew, I will marry you."

Present

From the drawer of the desk, I withdrew a small box made of ebony. It was intricately carved with a scene of a turbulent ocean and a lighthouse standing defiantly against a raging storm. Waves crashed against the shore, their foamy white caps frozen by the craftsman's skill.

I handed the box to Diane. "Go ahead, open it. But be careful. The contents are very delicate."

Diane, with a soft touch as though she were handling a newborn bird, took the box and examined the intricate design. Her fingers traced the chiseled waves and lighthouse, her eyes sparkling with curiosity. She turned it over in her hands carefully before finally lifting the delicate latch.

Inside, nestled within crimson velvet lining, was the seashell Andrew had used to propose to me that night at the lighthouse. It was an exquisite piece, a spiraled conch, as smooth as porcelain, with gentle hues of pink and cream.

Diane gasped as she laid eyes on the shell, her fingers hovering over it, afraid to touch it. "It's beautiful."

"Yes," I said, still marveling at it after all these years. "He went to the jewelry store the next day and bought me a proper ring, but this was the promise that started it all."

Diane gently closed the box, tears glistening in her eyes. "It sounds like a fairytale."

"In its own way, it was." I reached for the photo album on the table beside me, its leather cover worn with the years, pages filled with faded memories. I flipped it open to a page where a picture of a younger Andrew and I stood, wrapped in each other's arms, the lighthouse in the background. "We were so young and full of dreams. That lighthouse, the same one you see through the window over there, it was not just a place. It was the beginning of a journey together. That's why I had Andrew build our house here, so that we could look at the lighthouse anytime we wanted and remember how it all began."

"Love like yours is rare," she said softly. "I think I would have had that with Kyle. I only hope someday, when the time is right, that I can have that again."

"You're still young, Diane. There's plenty of time for you to find your own fairytale."

She gave me a half-hearted smile, but I could see sadness in her eyes. "Thank you," she said, her hands still gently cradling the precious box. "This is truly a story for the ages."

PART 3

CHAPTER 31

Saturday

Knowing Diane would be leaving tomorrow, I felt a strange mix of emotions. I should have been relieved that we'd reached the end of this journey, but instead, there was a lingering sadness, an unexpected yearning for more time together.

There was something about Diane that resonated with me. Something about her quiet courage, her stoic acceptance of the way life had panned out for her. Her stories, filled with drama and hardship, were told without self-pity or bitterness. They reflected a person bigger than the circumstance that had been thrust upon her, a person who was starting to make peace with her past.

I opened my eyes, squinting against the morning sun pouring in through the sheer curtains in my room. The delicate aroma of brewing coffee wafted up from the kitchen below, pulling me from my melancholic musings. I got up and ran a hand through my hair, steeling myself to face the day and its inevitable parting.

Downstairs, Diane and Judy were already in the kitchen, engrossed in a quiet conversation over coffee and scones. I watched them from the doorway, my presence unnoticed. Diane was laughing gently at something Judy had said, her eyes crinkling at the corners in a way that was so endearingly familiar. Her hands were wrapped around the coffee mug, fingers dancing lightly on the porcelain surface. For a fleeting moment, I wished I could freeze time and capture this moment forever in my memory. Since Judy's husband died, she hadn't laughed this way. There was a certain lightness now in the room, one that had been absent for far too long.

"Good morning." I finally announced my presence, and both women turned toward me, their faces lighting up with warm smiles.

"Good morning, sleepyhead," Judy teased. "Do you want some coffee?" she asked, already reaching for an empty mug.

"Yes, please," I said, moving over to the small breakfast nook. Diane moved over, allowing me room to sit. "I'm sorry for sleeping in. I suppose these last few days have been more tiring than I realized."

"No need for apologies. We all need rest. Besides, I'm here as long as you need me, so no rush."

Judy returned with my coffee, the steam swirling up from the dark liquid as she set it gently before me. I wrapped my hands around the warm mug, comforted by the familiar ritual.

"There are some scones left, if you're hungry," she added and nudged the plate toward me.

I picked one up and took a bite, the sweetness of the blueberries and hint of lemon zest taking me by surprise.

"Judy was just telling me how Rosie, after everything she'd been through, finally met a nice man and settled down."

Judy chimed in then. "Sorry if I stole some of your thunder."

"No, not at all," I said, waving her off with a laugh as I swallowed my mouthful of scone. "Besides, you know that part of the story better than I do anyway. You see, Diane, I wasn't around much during those days. After Andrew proposed, life came at us quickly, and things started to change."

Kitty Hawk, NC

February 1964

Although I had agreed to marry Andrew, we still hadn't decided on where we were going to live. So, for the first few months of our engagement, we lived in separate cities —he in Atlanta, and I in Kitty Hawk. We met in Charlotte as often as we could at a little bed and breakfast tucked away in the heart of the city. And it was there that we decided, with me going to law school in the fall, Chapel Hill would be our new home, a melting pot of new beginnings for the both of us.

Meanwhile, life returned to normal for Judy and Rosie. Rosie went back to work, and the restaurant, as it had before the trial, became a hive of activity. Judy put off her plans of moving to New York for another year to stay and help Rosie pick up the pieces of her life. It was during this time that Rosie met Hank.

Hank was a mechanic by trade who had moved from his hometown in Virginia to North Carolina in search of work. He had these kind, warm eyes, the sort that made you trust him immediately. He and Rosie hit it off from the start, and it wasn't long before talk of wedding bells began to circulate.

"I know what happened before," Rosie said to me and Judy one rainy afternoon, "but this feels like the real thing. Hank is... different." She was stirring her coffee, looking not into the cup but somewhere far beyond it. "I love him. I never thought I'd say that again—not after everything that happened with Peter."

We nodded sympathetically, our hands clasped around our

own cups of coffee. It seemed so long ago now, the memories of Peter's murder and Rosie's fight for her life. Peter, her first love, had been charming and charismatic. He'd swept her off her feet, only to reveal a dark side that led to his demise. His death had left a scar on Rosie's heart, one that we feared might never heal. But Hank, it seemed, had managed to mend the broken pieces of her heart.

"We're behind you, one hundred percent," said Judy, her voice steady and sure. "No matter what happens."

"Judy's right," I said, chiming in. "No matter what happens or where life takes us, we'll always be there for each other. We're not just friends, we're family."

Rosie's eyes swam with tears. "Thank you, both of you. I don't know what I would have done if it weren't for you two."

That afternoon was filled with emotion and reassurance that bridged the gap between our lives. We spoke of old times and future dreams—intertwining our lives in a way only true friends could.

As winter gave way to spring, then eventually to summer, I finally made up my mind about my future. Andrew was right—I was more than a waitress, destined for more than pouring coffee and serving up plates of fried fish and hushpuppies. So, I decided to enroll in law school at the University of North Carolina.

It was a bold move, one that both terrified and excited me. But it was time to find my own path, just as Rosie had found hers in love, and Judy had found hers in her restaurant.

When I finally broke the news to the girls that I would be leaving, I felt as if a weight had been lifted from my shoulders, a burden untied, released to drift into the ether.

"Law school?" Rosie gasped, her eyes widening with

surprise. "That's incredible, Sara. Congratulations!"

"Thanks." I turned to Judy, who sat quietly, brows furrowed. "I'm going to stay on until you find someone to replace me," I reassured her. "Andrew says we don't have to be in Chapel Hill until August, which gives you plenty of time. I hope you understand. This has nothing to do with you. You've been so kind to me, so supportive...but I need to do this for myself."

Judy didn't say anything at first, just sat there absorbing the news. "I know you do," she finally said. Her voice trembled as she continued. "Nothing stays the same forever, does it? People have to find their own paths." Judy looked back at me, eyes steady and understanding. "I'm just glad ours crossed for a while."

I nodded, tears pricking at my eyes. The small, cozy kitchen, the scent of cinnamon and sugar wafting from the oven, the faces of my friends etched with wisdom and kindness; all these would soon be memories. But I had to move forward. I reached across the table to take their hands.

"I will miss you both."

"Us, too," they replied, their hands tightening around mine.

"About the room upstairs," I said, gesturing toward the ceiling. "I assume you'll need me to move out soon, once you find my replacement."

Judy's eyes softened, the hint of a smile tugging at her lips. "You're welcome to stay as long as you like."

"Thank you, Judy," I said.

Judy waved her hand dismissively. "No thanks necessary," she said firmly, but her eyes were gentle. "We've been good for each other, Sara. You helped me more than you know. Honestly, if you hadn't come along when you did, I don't think I could have kept this place going."

At that moment, I realized how fickle fate could be. I'd left a hopeless situation, not knowing where I would land, only to find comfort and companionship in the unlikeliest of places. I had agreed to take a job and rent a room from a complete stranger and instead found a pillar of strength, a confidant, an unexpected ally. Judy had become my conduit of reassurance in a world turned upside down, my sanctuary in times of distress. The decision to leave suddenly seemed more daunting than I'd expected.

* * *

Six weeks later, I packed up my things and left Kitty Hawk. Andrew and I settled in an apartment in Durham, and school began soon after. It wasn't long before Judy decided to leave Kitty Hawk, too. After selling the restaurant to Rosie, she packed up her things and moved to New York to chase her dream of becoming a chef. Eventually, we all settled into our new routines, but it was never like it was before.

In the spring of 1965, Andrew and I were married in a chapel perched atop a hill overlooking the city. Rosalie and Hank tied the knot a month later in a ceremony on the beach. Judy was her maid of honor, and I was a bridesmaid. Soon after, Rosie became pregnant. And for a time, it looked as if everything was falling into place, as if the chapters of our lives were being written harmoniously by some grand cosmic author.

Present

"So, things worked out after all?" Diane asked as she

pushed her plate to the center of the table.

While I searched for the right response, Judy got up to clear the dishes and mentioned she had some errands to run in town. As soon as she left, I refocused on Diane's expectant smile.

"Yes and no," I said. "Things worked out, but not in the way any of us expected. When Rosie was five months pregnant, Hank was drafted into the army. From there, things only got worse. Shortly after arriving in Vietnam, while on patrol one morning, Hank was killed by a sniper. For a while, we feared Rosie might lose the baby from the stress, but she didn't. I guess some people just have a strength that defies understanding. Rosie was one of them. She held on with the tenacity of a mother bear protecting her cub, never allowing tragedy to break her spirit. On June twelfth, 1966, Rosie gave birth to a healthy baby girl whom she named Faith. So much tragedy had befallen Rosie that the birth of Faith seemed like a beacon of hope, a spark amidst the dark. But, as we would come to learn, sometimes life can be unpredictably cruel."

"Tell me nothing bad happened to Rosie," said Diane, looking as if she might cry. "Surely, life had taken enough from her. It owed her at least some happiness."

"Unfortunately, sometimes the world is a cruel place. And no matter how much it takes from us, it owes us nothing in return."

Diane's eyes welled up with tears, but she nodded, steeling herself for the worst.

"From the moment Rosie went into labor, there were complications. Despite the doctor's best efforts, the loss of blood was just too severe. She was able to hold her baby girl once, before she slipped into unconsciousness. A few hours later, Rosie was gone."

Diane gasped, her hand flying to her mouth. "Oh my God!"

"Judy and I were at her side until the very end. We held her hands, whispered encouragement, forced smiles onto our faces, so the last thing she saw wasn't fear or sadness. She made us promise to look after Faith, to give her the life she never got to live. We promised, of course, but the weight of that promise was almost too much for either of us. Judy took Rosie's death the hardest. After all, she and Rosie had been friends since they were kids. But even for me, having only known Rosie for a few years, the loss was almost unbearable. It felt like another chunk of my heart had been ripped out and cast into the abyss.

"That's awful," said Diane, blinking back tears.

"Yes, it was. But we couldn't let ourselves get consumed by our grief. Faith needed us. And if there's one thing that Rosie taught us, it's that life goes on, no matter what." I took a breath, pausing to collect my thoughts before continuing. "Things moved quickly after that. With Rosie having no family to speak of, the state had to intercede. They took the baby into their care, promising that they'd do right by the little one. Judy tried to fight it, and so did I. She wanted to adopt the child herself, but social services wouldn't allow it. I asked Andrew if there was anything he could do, but it was beyond his control. And so Faith was taken from us, never to be seen again." Tears fell unwillingly from my eyes, a waterfall of sorrow. Even after all these years, the pain felt just as raw.

Diane stared at me, her eyes wide with shock. "I can't believe they took her like that. Couldn't they see that the child was better off with the people who loved her?"

I shrugged, my heart heavy. "Unfortunately, there are rules for these sorts of situations. The state cares about legality, not love." I turned and gazed out the window, watching the rain trickle down the glass. It was as if the heavens, too, were weeping for Rosie and her little Faith.

"How does anyone get over something like that?" Diane asked, shaking her head in disbelief.

"Slowly," I answered, remembering the grief that had engulfed us in the weeks following Rosie's passing. "Very slowly. And you never really get over it. You just learn to live with it. But I find solace in the thought of that little girl who was taken from us too early. Even though we don't know what became of her, I'd like to think she's out there somewhere, living her best life, unaware of the tragedy that marked her earliest days. Rosie would have wanted that for her, a chance at happiness unshadowed by the past. Still, it's hard not to dwell on what might have been."

We sat quietly, both of us lost in our own thoughts, neither of us knowing quite what to say.

"What happened next? When did you decide to move back to Kitty Hawk?"

"After I finished law school, Andrew and I moved to Asheville, where we opened a practice of our own. There, I met a man by the name of Owen Simmons. He was a wealthy businessman who also happened to be a lover of literature. He and I became good friends. Little did I know that a few years later, he would become governor. Soon after he took office, he offered me the position of judge for the Outer Banks District. I accepted immediately. It felt like an opportunity to finally do some good, to prevent tragedies like Faith's from happening again. That's when we moved back to Kitty Hawk, the pull of the ocean too strong to resist. And thus began another chapter of my life."

"And you've been here ever since?"

I nodded. "Ever since."

"What about Sims Chapel. Did you ever go back?"

"Not to Sims Chapel. But I went to see my mother several times in Rogersville," I replied, recalling those trips across the mountains. "The last was in the winter of 1973, to attend her funeral. But after that, no. I never went back."

"What about Jack? Did you ever see or talk to him again?"

I shook my head. "I kinda thought he might show up for Mother's funeral, but he didn't. In fact, I remember rehearsing what I'd say to him if I saw him, but fortunately it never came to that."

"Is that something you regret?"

"What? Not seeing him again? Or not being able to say to him all the things I'd rehearsed?"

"Either. Or both."

I shrugged. "I guess a part of me has always wanted to see him again, to make amends for what I did. But the more time goes by, the more I realize the past should just stay there."

Diane took a breath and cleared her expression before going on. "So, where do you go from here? What's next on the docket for the Honorable Sara Hastings?"

I chuckled lightly, my gaze drifting toward the window, the darkened skies offering me no answers. "Ah, now that's the million-dollar question, isn't it?" I ran a hand through my hair, the weight of age catching up with me momentarily. "I'm not as young as I used to be, or as sharp. The adventures I seek now are not quite as thrilling as they were in my youth. But the quest for justice? That's a journey I'll never tire of. And there are still battles to fight right here at home."

"Like what?"

"There's the fight against inequality, for one. There's the issue of homelessness that still plagues our town. And don't get me started on the educational gaps in our school systems." I paused, the ice clinking against my glass as I took a long sip of my drink. "Beyond that, I don't know. I try to live each day as it comes, not worry too much about the future. I've always believed that if you try to do good every day, the future will sort itself out."

"That's a pretty philosophical outlook," Diane noted, scribbling down something in her notepad. "Does that kind of wisdom come with age?"

I laughed. "I suppose it does. As you age, you tend to see the bigger picture. The petty things that would bother you when you were younger seem insignificant when you're older."

"Does that mean you've made peace with your past?"

"Yes," I answered carefully. But even as I said it, I could feel the sting of doubt. I quickly squashed it down with a swig of my drink. "I've made peace with the fact that there are some things in my past I can't change. The mistakes I've made, they're a part of me now. I've had to learn to live with that."

CHAPTER 32

Feeling slightly weak, I suggested we break for lunch, and Diane readily agreed. We moved to the solarium, where we nibbled on sandwiches Judy had prepared earlier that morning and sipped on iced tea. Our conversation shifted to lighter topics. We discussed the weather and the change in seasons. Diane was particularly fond of fall, a sentiment I shared.

"I just love the crisp feeling in the air," said Diane. "But it's the colors I love most of all. The rich reds and deep oranges. The world feels like it's on fire, but in the most beautiful way. Cassie loves it too, especially now that we have a dog. We all go on walks together in the evenings when I get home from work."

"I imagine Cassie is missing you this week. I'm sure you're anxious to get home to see her, aren't you?"

"I am. You know, I was lying in bed last night, thinking. This is the longest I've ever been apart from her." She paused for a moment, watching a squirrel as it darted across the lawn, its bushy tail flicking wildly. "I wish she could have seen this place. She would have loved it, especially the ocean. She's never been."

"Then you'll have to bring her by for a visit the next time you're out this way. You're both welcome here anytime."

"Thank you. That's very kind of you."

There was a pause in our conversation as we both took comfort in the peaceful silence of the old house. It had a way of soaking up noise, leaving only the pleasant hum of quiet at midday.

After finishing lunch, Diane and I stepped out to get some fresh air and took a walk around the property. She marveled at the beautiful gardens and the various fruit trees scattered throughout. We made our way down to the beach, where we watched the waves crash against the shore and seagulls swooping down to catch fish.

"I noticed the little sign hanging on the gate leading to the cottage— 'Rosie's Place.' Did you put it there in her memory?"

"I wanted that cottage to be a place where I could go to not only think about the present and future, but also the past. And there was no one more important to my past than Rosie. So, I had that little sign put there on the gate to remind me of her. I know it sounds silly, but somehow I feel closer to her when I'm there."

"It doesn't sound silly," she said, her gaze drifting toward the distant cottage. "It sounds like love."

We walked on, each lost in our own thoughts. The beach was empty except for us and a lone seagull cawing overhead.

"You know, when I saw that picture of the three of you, I felt a connection to Rosie, as if she was trying to tell me something. I get that way sometimes. Like, when I was younger, I always felt like there was this presence, someone watching over me, leading me toward something. It's hard to explain but seeing that picture brought back the same feeling."

"I feel that way sometimes, too. I would like to believe that Rosie is indeed there somewhere, still watching over me and Judy." My eyes drifted toward the horizon, where the ocean and the sky merged into one. "That brings me a sense of comfort, and in a strange way, it feels like a piece of her is still here."

As we made our way back up to the house, Diane suddenly

stopped in her tracks and turned toward me.

"Can I ask you something personal?"

"Of course."

"Do you ever dream about her?"

"All the time," I admitted, a wistful smile etching across my face as countless memories flooded my mind. "I dream of her laughter, her touch, the way she used to dance around the kitchen when she was cooking. I dream of her feisty spirit and her gentle heart."

"I dream of my mother sometimes," Diane said as we stepped up onto the back porch. "Even though I never met her, I have this image in my mind of what I think she may have looked like. Her hair, her face, her eyes. I think they would have been brown, like mine."

"I think that's beautiful," I replied, feeling a deep connection to Diane in that moment.

"Oh," Diane said, her expression brightening as if she had just remembered something. "I forgot to ask if you and Andrew ever had any children. I didn't see any pictures in the house."

The question brought a wave of emotion washing over me. "No, we didn't. We tried for a while, but...it just never happened." I paused, allowing myself to confront the hidden sorrow that lingered in the corners of my heart.

"I'm sorry," said Diane, her voice holding a tinge of remorse. "I didn't mean to bring up a sensitive subject."

I shook my head, mustering up a small smile. "It's all right. Some people just aren't meant to have children. And Andrew and I lived a fulfilling life together. We enjoyed each other's company, traveled to places I only dreamed of as a kid, and we poured our love into the world in our own ways. We had each other, and that was enough. Besides, it may have been a blessing in disguise.

"How so?"

I took a deep breath, collecting my thoughts. "I'm going to tell you something, but you must promise not to say anything to anyone else. And you can't write about it."

"Okay," she replied, a look of worry etched into the lines around her eyes. "I promise."

"When you first arrived, you asked me why I wanted to tell my story, why now. The truth is, I'm sick, and I don't know how much time I have left before my mind starts to deteriorate."

Diane's face fell, taking a moment to find the right words. "It's Huntington's, isn't it?"

I nodded, not trusting my voice. "Yes," I finally managed to whisper. "The same disease that took my mother, and her mother before her. The same disease that will someday take me."

"Does Judy know?"

I nodded. "Yes, she knows. She's been a wonderful support, helping me with doctor's appointments, medication... everything really."

Diane took my hand in hers, her touch gentle and warm. "I'm so sorry."

"Don't be. I've had a wonderful life. Longer and better than many, and certainly more than I ever hoped for. Yes, the ending is bitter, but it's not the ending that matters, is it? It's the journey, and mine has been quite the adventure. And that's why I think Andrew and I not being able to have children is a blessing. I would have hated myself had I brought a child into this world, only to pass this affliction onto them."

Diane nodded, her eyes glossy with unshed tears. "That's a brave perspective to have," she said.

I shrugged. "Perhaps. Or maybe it's just a woman trying to make sense of the hand she's been dealt, trying to see a silver lining in an otherwise cloudy sky."

CHAPTER 33

Traversing the long hallway that led back to the center of the house, Diane turned to me, her expression serious yet gentle. "If I haven't said so already, you're one of the strongest women I've ever met. I mean after all the ups and downs with Jack, and more recently with your diagnosis and the loss of your husband, you still stand tall, still find a way to smile. You are extraordinary."

I gave a thin, appreciative smile, nodding slightly as we entered the foyer. "Speaking of Andrew, it's funny, he's been gone almost nine months, and I still find myself expecting him to come through the door any moment, with that mischievous grin of his and a story to make me laugh. It's so eerie how an absence can feel so much like a presence."

We rounded the corner and walked toward the grand staircase, its wooden balustrade reflecting the soft glow of the chandelier overhead.

"In my experience, that's how it feels when you lose someone so deeply woven into the fabric of your life," said Diane. "The heart takes time to reconcile with the mind's truth."

Turning left, we stepped into the library and settled in for the final time. My story was nearly complete, but there were still a few loose ends to tie up, a few pieces of the puzzle missing.

"Do you have any regrets?" Diane asked when she was ready.

Regrets. I had more than a few, but I decided to focus on

the one that weighed the most heavily on my heart. "Just one. I wish I'd been able to find out what happened to Rosie's child. Considering the promise Judy and I made, it'd be nice to know that she found a good home, that she was loved and cherished. But I guess some mysteries are destined to remain unsolved."

"Speaking of mysteries, did they ever figure out who really killed Peter Sullivan?"

"Yes. It was Graham Walden, Peter's associate. A few months after Rosie was set free, the FBI tracked him down and arrested him at a bar in Boston. As it turned out, Graham had been stealing from Peter for years. When Peter found out, he confronted Graham and that's when Graham killed him."

"Good heavens. And he was ready to let Rosie take the fall for his crime? How despicable."

"I often think about the circumstances of that case, and I have mixed feelings about the whole thing."

"What do you mean?"

"If Peter hadn't been killed, Rosie would never have been charged with his murder. If that hadn't happened, Andrew would never have come to Kitty Hawk, he'd never have asked me to work for him, and I would never have fallen in love with him or the law. So, in some respects, Peter's death was the catalyst for my life taking a completely different, better direction. Ironic, isn't it?" I took a sip of tea before continuing. "But then, I wonder if things would have been better if Peter Sullivan had never come into our lives. I think about Judy and myself. Where would we be today? What would we be doing? But mostly, I think about Rosie, and I can't help but wonder if she'd still be with us."

Diane nodded, a faraway look clouding her eyes. "If you could do it all over again—start from the beginning—would you change anything?"

It was a question I had asked myself a thousand times. I'd often thought about the little white lies I'd told along the way, the moments when I should have spoken, or the times I spoke when perhaps saying nothing at all was the wiser choice. I'd considered every possible scenario at one time or another, but I always came to the same conclusion. "Actually, I don't think I'd change a thing," I finally said. "Every decision, every mistake, every moment of joy and heartache... They've all shaped me into who I am today."

Diane smiled at that,. "And what is that, may I ask? Who are you today? Are you really the 'Iron Lady' as many of your contemporaries claim?"

I took a moment, my wrinkled hands resting on the table between us. "No. I am not made of iron. Iron may be strong but it's not flexible. It cracks under pressure, rusts, and decays with time. I've weathered storms that threatened to tear me apart, yet here I am, still standing. I've bent but never broken, scarred but never shattered. I am a beacon of hope for those who have lost their way...and a reminder of the past for those who dare to forget. No, I am not iron. I am a survivor."

"Just like the lighthouse," said Diane, her gaze shifting to the window, where the silhouette of the structure was visible in the evening haze. "A sentinel, standing tall in the face of the storm."

"Yes," I said, chuckling at the thought. "I suppose I am."

Diane turned off the recorder and closed her notebook. After she'd put her things in her satchel, she looked up at me and said, "As much as I hate for this to end, I think I have all I need. It'll take some time to organize my notes and write a first draft, but I should have something for you to look at by

Christmas. Thank you again, for everything. This week has been an unforgettable journey. Your story is truly remarkable."

With a nod, I got up, my joints creaking from the weight of my years. "You're welcome, dear. I'm just glad my story will finally be told. I hope it makes a difference to someone out there."

We walked to the door together, our footsteps echoing in the hollow space.

"Are you sure you don't want to join me for dinner?" Diane asked as she opened the door.

"Thank you, but no. I have some correspondence I need to catch up on. Besides, I want you to experience the pier the way I once did, unfiltered, untouched by my tales. It has a magic of its own. But I can't wait to hear your thoughts when you get home this evening."

Diane nodded and set off for her car. When she was gone, I wandered through the cavernous old mansion, each room filled with memories so thick it was as if I could reach out and touch them. The grandeur of the ballroom, now faded with time, still held traces of the glittering parties of my youth. The study, once a hub of intellectual discourse and strategic planning, was now silent save for the ticking of the grandfather clock that stood in the corner. The many bedrooms, each with their own unique stories, lay quiet and cold, their time of lodging long past.

I reached the nursery last, the room I dared not step foot in for fear of the ghosts that lingered there. It was the room where my dreams had once lived and died, a sacred space left unfulfilled. The painted pastels now faded into a dull gray, the crib covered in dust, empty and echoing with silent lullabies. It was in this room I allowed myself to be enveloped by the past, my heart heavy with the weight of what could have been.

The tiny brass rocking horse, a relic from a hopeful shopping trip decades prior, sat motionless on the dusty chest of drawers. I picked it up, turning it over in my hands, the cool metal a reminder of lost time. A single tear traced its way down my wrinkled cheek, landing softly on the golden mane. I allowed myself that singular moment of grief, a penance for the choices I had made. I placed the horse back on its perch, its tarnished form catching a sliver of dying sunlight bleeding in through the window.

Closing the door, I turned back toward the heart of the house, feeling a chill seep into the bones of the old mansion. As I passed through the grand foyer, I could almost hear Andrew's voice calling me to dinner, ready to compare case notes or regale me with another of his misadventures from law school.

Once I'd settled into the library, I thought about the week, and all that Diane and I had shared with one another. Her probing questions had forced me to delve into the darkest corners of my memory, to relive joys and sorrows alike. A lifetime of secrets, spilled like an overturned glass of wine, staining the pristine tablecloth of my solitude. It was the first time in my life that I had divulged so much, had gone through all the years, all the heartaches, and all the triumphs, from start to finish. And as I leaned back in my chair, taking a moment to reflect, I felt a strange release, like a bird finally breaking free. I had spent so many years caged by my past, and now, like the old mansion that surrounded me, it, too, was crumbling, leaving behind only the echoes of what once was.

Judy returned a little after six, her face pale and expression panicked.

"Judy, what's the matter?"

Judy took a deep breath, her hands shaking as she reached

into her pocket and pulled out a photograph. "Something you need to see."

The photograph was old and worn, but the image was clear. It was of Rosie and her baby, taken minutes after she had given birth.

"Where did you find this?" I asked, believing that the pictures we had taken that day were lost to time.

"In a box I had tucked away in the attic, hidden under years of dust."

I stared at the photograph again. Rosie was smiling, her eyes full of love and exhaustion. The baby, swaddled tightly in a blanket, slept peacefully in her arms. It was difficult to look at, knowing that a few hours after that picture had been taken, Rosie had died of complications. Making it all the more painful was the fact that the baby had disappeared soon after, swallowed up by the system and never seen again.

"Why are you showing me this?" I asked, the pain of that day suddenly rekindling.

"Look closer."

I squinted at the photograph again, this time scanning every minute detail. My breath caught as the realization dawned. "Oh my God!" My heart began to pound in my chest. "You don't think...?"

Judy nodded, her gaze holding the same the shock that was now coursing through me. "Yes," she said, her voice barely a whisper. "Look at the baby's right ear. The birthmark...it's identical to..."

"To Diane's," I said, my thoughts racing. "But...how can that be?" I couldn't believe what I was implying, what Judy was hinting at.

"I think Diane is Rosie's daughter," she said. "I think she's the one we've been searching for all these years."

My mind was spinning, caught in a whirlwind of thoughts and feelings. The truth was so close, yet it seemed almost impossible to grasp.

"No," I finally said, not wanting to believe. "It can't be." But even as I said it, I couldn't deny the evidence, the stark reality glaring back at me. A chill of dread seeped deep into my bones. "Are you sure?" I asked, clinging to the last remnants of disbelief.

Judy simply nodded, her gaze steady and resolute. "I've never been more sure of anything in my life."

The room suddenly seemed to spin as the weight of Judy's words settled on my shoulders. My hand moved instinctively to the kitchen table, fingertips brushing against the cold wood, grounding me in the moment that threatened to shatter my reality. The photograph shook slightly in my grasp, the edges crinkling under the tension of my fingers. A web of denial, shock, and disbelief coiled tightly in the pit of my stomach. My mind ached with a thousand questions, each one more incriminating than the last.

"Then..." I started, my voice shaky with the burden of realization, "We need to talk to her, she deserves to know the truth."

Judy nodded in agreement. "But we must tread carefully. News like this could shatter her world, and we don't know how she'll react."

CHAPTER 34

It was dark when Diane's headlights appeared on the horizon. I had been at the window, watching the empty road, anxiously awaiting her return. Now that the news of her identity had sunk in, I felt a mixture of excitement and fear coursing through my veins. The woman I had come to know was in truth Rosie's daughter. It was a truth too extraordinary to grasp, yet it was all too real now.

As Diane's car pulled into the driveway, a cloud of dust pluming behind it, I felt my heart pound in my chest. The porch light illuminated her silhouette as she stepped out of the car. I glanced at Judy, who was sitting on the stairs, her hands clenched tightly in her lap.

"You were right," Diane said as she stepped into the foyer. "That place is something else. And it has the best fish and hushpuppies I've ever had." She shrugged out of her coat and hung it in on the rack beside the door. "What is it?" she asked, her eyes darting between Judy and me. "Why do you both look like you've seen a ghost?" She gave a challenging smile, her eyes glinting with curiosity.

That look. The way she tilted her head to the side and narrowed her eyes, a playful smirk tugging at the corners of her lips. It was all so familiar, so deeply engraved in my memory that it felt like déjà vu. In that moment, I realized that Diane wasn't just some stranger that had wandered into our lives by accident. No, this was something more. Something profoundly serendipitous.

Judy stepped to my side, her fingers curling around my arm. Her breath hitched as Diane tilted her head to the other side, her smirk morphing into a grin that sent shivers down my spine. The room suddenly felt too small, the walls closing in on us as Diane stood there, still as a statue.

For a moment, I was transported back to when Rosie was more than just a memory. To a time when it was the three of us against the world. Judy's grip on my arm tightened further, pulling me back to the present.

"There's something we need to tell you," I began, my voice trembling ever so slightly. I could feel Judy's fingers dig into my arm as a reassurance, but her eyes were wide with trepidation.

"Sounds serious," Diane remarked, crossing the room to take a seat on the plump armchair near the fireplace. Her playful grin had vanished, replaced with a thoughtful, almost reflective expression. Her eyes met mine, an unspoken question hanging between us. Judy's grip on my arm loosened a bit as she took a step back, giving me the space to speak.

"You told me once that you wished you knew the color of your mother's eyes. Do you remember?"

Diane nodded slowly, a hint of confusion creeping into her eyes. "Yes, I do. Why?"

I swallowed, feeling the words rise in my throat like a tide. "They were brown, sweetheart. Your mother's eyes were brown."

Diane's eyes widened just slightly, her gaze flickered between Judy and me, her mind seemed to be racing. "Excuse me?"

I could see her trying to piece together the puzzle, trying to make sense of our cryptic words. "Is this some sort of joke?"

I swallowed again, trying to calm the storm inside me. This was it, the moment that fate had been leading us to. "No, dear. This is no joke."

"We knew your mother," Judy spoke up, her voice steady despite the gravity of the situation. "We knew her very well."

Diane's fingers tightened around the edge of the armchair, her knuckles going white. She shook her head in denial, in confusion, in an attempt to push away the words we were throwing at her. "I don't understand," she managed to choke out. "How could you possibly...?" Suddenly, her voice trailed off as something in her eyes sparked. A realization —or perhaps an acceptance —that gradually spread from the depths of her gaze to the tilt of her mouth. "Rosie," she said, whispering the name. "Rosie was my mother, wasn't she?"

"Yes," I breathed out, the word lodged heavy in my throat. "She was. And she loved you very much."

Diane's lips trembled, tears beginning to pool in the corners of her eyes. She nodded slowly, taking this revelation in stride, or at least attempting to. "Why didn't you tell me?"

"Because, we didn't know for sure until just now."

Diane looked up at me, a myriad of emotions flashing across her face. "And how can you be so sure?"

"Because of the way you smile," Judy said softly. "It's the same smile Rosie used to have."

"And because of this," I reached into my sweater pocket and pulled out the old, faded photograph. "This is you, Diane. And this is your mother."

Diane took the picture with trembling hands, her gaze devouring the image. She traced the baby's features, the curve of Rosie's smile. Instinctively, her hand went to the birthmark below her ear, her fingers lightly tracing over the familiar indentation as if touching it could somehow bridge the years of separation. She looked so vulnerable in that moment, lost in a world that had just been flipped on its axis.

For a moment, she stayed silent, her eyes flickering between the photograph and us. "Why?" she finally whispered. "Why am I only now finding out about this?"

"I don't know," I began. "I spent the majority of my career searching for you, but every route I pursued led to a dead end. I had all but given up hope, until Judy found that picture."

"And when we saw that birthmark...we knew it was you," said Judy.

Diane looked down at the photograph once more, her eyes lingering on her mother's smiling face. "She was beautiful, wasn't she?"

"Yes, she was," said Judy, reaching out to touch Diane's arm. "She loved you so much, Diane. The last thing she ever said to me...her last words...were your name."

A tremor seemed to pass through Diane's body as she absorbed Judy's words. A single tear escaped from the corner of her eye and traced a path down her cheek. "I...I'm not sure what to do now," she said, still clutching the photograph.

"Take your time, Diane. There's no need to rush this," I advised gently. Her shoulders relaxed slightly at my words, but the confusion was still evident in her eyes.

Judy shifted beside me, reaching into her bag. "Rosie left something for you. We thought you should have it." She handed Diane a small, velvet box. Diane opened the battered box tentatively and inside, nested on a bed of old, discolored silk was a heart-shaped locket. The necklace was made of gold and had intricate carvings on its surface—tiny, delicate roses that were so finely crafted they seemed to bloom from the metal. She held it up to the light, mesmerized by the way it glowed.

"Open it," Judy encouraged softly, her gaze fixed on Diane's face. Suddenly apprehensive, Diane complied, revealing a tiny, faded photograph of her mother, Rosie, and her father, Hank. "I look like them," she choked out between sobs.

"Yes, you do," Judy replied, her tone gentle. "You've got your mother's eyes, and your father's smile."

As Diane studied the faces in the locket, a faint smile tugged at the corners of her lips. Her fingers traced the edge of her father's image. "He was handsome," she whispered, more to herself than to us. "And they look so...happy."

"They were," Judy confirmed. "Very much so." I could see a tear forming in Judy's eye as she recalled the past, her features softening with remembrance. "They were hopelessly in love and overjoyed to have you."

Diane closed her eyes, the tears flowing freely now. She clutched the locket tighter, as if holding onto her parents' memory. "Thank you," she said, her red-rimmed eyes meeting ours, "for this. You have no idea how much this means to me."

When Diane set off for the cottage, Judy and I could finally breathe again.

"We did a good thing tonight," Judy said as she handed me a glass of wine.

"Yes, we did," I agreed, sipping the sweet liquid while my gaze followed Diane's retreating figure. "But it's only a start. There's so much more she needs to know."

"You're right. And in time, we'll tell her everything."

"I was thinking," I said, staring off into the darkness, "about asking her to stay."

"At the cottage?" Judy asked, her eyebrows knitting together in surprise.

"Yes," I replied firmly. "She said she's always dreamed of living by the ocean, and what better spot is there anywhere in the world than right here? Besides, we could both use the company."

Judy took a moment to consider it, her expression inscrutable. "It's a big commitment, you know. We'd be taking on an important role in her life, not to mention that of her daughter's. Are we ready for that?"

I looked at Judy, my eyes steady, my voice brimming with conviction. "I've never been more ready for anything in my life."

CHAPTER 35

When the lights in the cottage had gone out, Judy and I took the path that led to the lighthouse, our shoes crunching on the fine shells under the inky blackness of night. Judy wore her favorite red jacket, the one that matched the rusty hue of her hair and clung to my arm. Every now and then, I stole a glance at her, wondering what thoughts were tumbling through her mind.

As we crested the hill, the lighthouse came into view, standing tall and proud as it always had. We stopped short of it, our gazes drawn to a pair of headstones nestled in the sand. For a long time, we stood there, neither of us saying a word. One of the headstones was weathered, the name and date etched into it barely visible under the moonlight. But the other one was relatively new, its polished marble surface reflecting the pale light.

The inscription read, "Andrew Hastings, 1929 - 1993," and beneath it a small quote, "To the lighthouse, my love."

I let go of Judy's arm and approached the grave, laying a single red rose atop it. "I miss you," I whispered, my voice swallowed by the roar of the nearby ocean. "But I'm surviving, just like always."

When it was Judy's turn, she knelt down in front of the other headstone. She brushed away the sand and a few fallen leaves, her finger tracing the faded lettering of Rosie's name. "We did it, doll," she said. "We found Faith. Your little girl is safe and sound, just like you wanted." Her voice wavered through her tears, raw with emotion. "We promised we would never forget. And we haven't."

As if on cue, the lighthouse's beam swung in our direction, piercing the night. It cast long, eerie shadows over the graves, making the headstones seem taller. The light seemed almost tangible, as if we could reach out our hands and touch it.

Judy's hand found mine, her fingers trembling slightly. "I think she would have been happy with how things turned out, don't you?"

I squeezed her hand reassuringly, thinking back to the stories that Rosalie had written, with their surprising and satisfying endings. "Yes," I said, nodding my head. "I don't think she could have written it any better herself."

* * *

At dawn, I walked down to the cottage to see if Diane was awake. The light in the living room window was already glowing, illuminating the dew-kissed grass. I could see her hunched over a notepad at the coffee table, forehead creased with concentration. Her lips moved slightly as though she were whispering the words to herself.

My approach was quiet, but she must have sensed me because she looked up as I stepped onto the porch.

"Oh, it's you," she said, opening the door for me. "For a minute there, I thought it was some early morning wanderer." She smiled. "Need a cup of coffee?"

"Please," I said, settling into the worn leather armchair by the hearth. Diane padded to the kitchen and poured two cups, handing one to me.

"What brings you here so early?" she asked, sitting down

on the edge of the sofa.

I took a sip of coffee, letting the warm, bitter flavor work its magic before answering. "I was thinking...since I've got this perfectly good cottage going to waste, and since you're going to have thousands of questions now, maybe you could use it? I mean, if you want to."

She looked at me with surprise. "I don't understand."

"I'm asking you to come live with me...you and Cassie, in the cottage. It doesn't have to be forever, just until you get the answers you're looking for, or until you decide it's time to move on."

"That's very kind of you, but I could never afford a place like this."

I chuckled, shaking my head. "It's not about affording it, Diane. I'm offering it to you, no strings attached. This place was always meant for someone like you, someone who can appreciate its beauty and its solitude. Besides, you'll need a space like this if you're to write the next great American novel."

Diane took a deep breath, her fingers lightly tracing the rim of her coffee cup. "You're serious, aren't you?"

"Very much so," I replied, shifting in my chair to face her more directly. "I'm not asking you to decide today. Just think about—"

"I'll take it," she said, cutting me off.

Her sudden response took me aback, but then a slow grin spread across my face. I felt like I was dreaming. "Don't you want to talk it over with Cassie first? And what about your job at the newspaper?"

She waved her hand dismissively, "Cassie will be thrilled. She's always wanted to see the beach. And as for the newspaper... It was never supposed to be a long-term gig. Besides, if I need to make a little money while I'm cultivating my career as a novelist, I might wander down to the pier and get a waitressing job. I know several great women who got their start there."

CHAPTER 36

3 Weeks Later

"Are you sure you don't need us to go with you?" Judy asked, standing in the doorway as I lugged a bag out to the trunk of my car.

I glanced back over my shoulder, finding the three of them—Judy, Diane, and Cassie—standing in the doorway. "Thank you, but I'll be fine. It's just for a couple of days, and I really need to do this on my own."

"Call us when you get there," said Diane. "You know how this one worries," she said, thumbing toward Cassie.

I chuckled as I shut the trunk, giving them all a reassuring smile. "I will, I promise."

Crossing the mountains from North Carolina into Tennessee, I was met with a feeling of familiarity, the kind one gets when returning home after many years. Over the years, I'd reminded myself that I no longer belonged to these mountains. Yet, as I drove down the winding roads, I felt an old kinship rekindled. This place had changed, but so had I.

But there was a part of me that knew this was no longer my home, that the roots I had once laid down here were long since torn up and transplanted. But the familiar scent of honeysuckle and pine, the echoing calls of the herons, and the rolling blue-green peaks of the Smoky Mountains themselves seemed to plead with me otherwise.

For hours, I drove around the lake, reacquainting myself with the area. I passed by the weathered sign of the old Miller's farm, where Jack and I used to steal apples on lazy summer afternoons. The fields were now overgrown with weeds, rebellious against their former glory. The farmhouse itself stood defiant against the passage of time, its paint peeling off in places like the skin of a snake.

I visited my childhood home, where so many of my memories were born and nurtured. For a long time, I stared at it from a distance, absorbing the sight of the sagging porch and the wild tendrils of ivy that had claimed the side wall. The once-green lawn, where I had spent countless summer days running around daydreaming, was now an unkempt patchwork of wild grass and dandelions. Even the garden, where Mama once tended her roses, was now swallowed up by neglect.

After a few moments of bittersweet reflection, I continued to the dock, where I had once worked and laughed under the summer sun. I knew I shouldn't, but I just had to see it, to connect with the memory of my first love. But as I pulled into the parking lot, I was struck by how drastically it had changed. Gone were the rickety wooden planks that creaked under our weight, replaced by sturdy concrete. Even the bait shop, where once we'd spent hours picking out the best worms and minnows, was now a lakeside café.

Amid the changes, the old boathouse stood, albeit precariously, crooked on its foundation. Its paint, once a vibrant white, had succumbed to the elements and was now a haunting shade of gray, peeling away in large strips.

For a moment, I stood there, watching the water dance against the old, rotted pillars of the dock. The lake was still a deep shade of blue, reflecting the cloudless sky above. And when I closed my eyes, I could almost hear our laughter, the splashes as we jumped off the edge into the cool depths below.

Then I saw him. Jack. He was leaning against the boathouse, gazing into the distance with that familiar faraway look. It was the same man I had once known, weathered by the cruel hands of time. The sight of him after all these years, a living, breathing echo of my youth, stirred in me a wellspring of emotions too complex to define. A fusion of joy, sadness, nostalgia, and a sense of longing cut through my heart like a knife. His hair was touched by silver now, a stark contrast to the sandy-brown waves I remembered running my fingers through, and his skin bore the creases of years lived hard and fully. His hands were hardened by labor, veins prominent under the sun-baked skin. Despite the years, his smiled was unchanged, still that teasing, boyish grin that had once set my heart aflame.

My instinct was to run to him, to tell him that I was sorry, to ask for his forgiveness. But the weight of years and choices held me in place. I watched him pull out an old ball cap from his back pocket and put it on, shielding his eyes from the sun.

I mouthed his name, needing to feel the sound of it on my lips, to remember what it felt like to call out to him. He stiffened, as if he had heard me, turned and looked in my direction. But he didn't seem to see me. His eyes scanned past me, roaming over the landscape, and it was as though I were a ghost. A single tear escaped my eye, tracing a warm path down my cold cheek. Whether he didn't recognize me or was simply lost in his own memories, I couldn't say.

Returning to my car, I took one last glance at the figure by the boathouse. Jack was nothing more than a silhouette now, his figure merging with the growing shadows as the sun dipped low in the western sky.

Having gotten what I came for, I pulled away, leaving him, the lake, and shared memories behind me. I could have stopped there ... could have gotten back on the interstate and headed east until I saw the coast, but there was one final piece of business I needed to settle.

Finally, I arrived at the place I had been dreading most. Turning up the long drive, I braced myself for the wave of emotions that were sure to come. I could already see the big, imposing structure of the old home standing stoically against the evening sky. Jack's house on the hill.

Stepping out of the car, I took in the house that had once belonged to Clara. The façade was still as grand as ever, with its towering columns, gleaming bay windows, and the intricate lattice of ivy creeping up the aged walls. In contrast, the front yard was bursting with an array of shrubs and flowers, illuminated by the warm glow of evening light. An old stone path, carpeted with moss, led me toward the entrance of the house.

As I stepped up onto the porch, the wooden planks creaked, echoing memories of countless afternoons spent with Clara and Ellie, sipping lemonade and sweet tea, during that summer so long ago. With a deep breath, I raised my hand in a fist and knocked on the door.

After a few seconds, the door squeaked open to reveal a woman whose once lively eyes now bore the weight of time.

"Sara?" said Ellie, her voice trembling with disbelief. "Is it really you?" Her once dark brown hair was now a soft, faded auburn, with streaks of white shining in the late afternoon sun. She wore a simple floral dress, the kind she had always favored, even when we were girls. It hung loosely on her slender frame, the vibrant patterns a stark contrast to the years etched into her face.

"Yes, Ellie," I replied. "It's me. Listen, I hate to barge in on you like this, but I was in the area and was hoping we could talk."

Ellie blinked slowly, seemingly processing the unexpected apparition on her doorstep. The lines across her forehead deepened, and she opened her mouth to speak but then closed it again. "Of course," she finally stammered out, stepping back to allow me entry into the foyer.

The door swung shut behind me, the familiar scent of cedar wood and dried lavender enveloping me. It was a fragrance intertwined with laughter, secrets, and comforting reassurances from days long gone. The dimly lit hallway stretched out before me, lined with old family portraits—some of Jack and Ellie, and others with their daughter. They seemed to watch over the house with a sense of timeless vigilance.

For a moment, I stood there, letting the nostalgia wash over me. As I walked further in, my eyes were drawn to one portrait. It was of us—me, Clara, and Ellie—taken the summer when Ellie came to stay, the summer everything changed. I wondered why she had kept it all these years. Perhaps it reminded her of simpler times, before the complications of life had set in. Regardless, there it was, as if waiting for my return.

A soft rustling sound brought me back from my reverie. Ellie had disappeared into the kitchen, emerging with two glasses of sweet tea.

"This is for you," said Ellie.

I took the glass, my hands shaking a bit. "Thank you."

Ellie nodded, gesturing to the worn leather sofa in the living room. "Please, sit," she said, her tone gentle and inviting.

Together, we moved to the living room, our steps slow and cautious as if any sudden movement might shatter the fragile peace we had found in our reunion.

I eased myself onto the supple, time-worn leather, as Ellie did the same. I sipped my sweet tea, letting it calm my nerves. Ellie sat opposite me, cradling her glass in her hands, an unreadable expression on her face.

"So, what brings you this way?" Ellie asked.

I set my glass on the worn oak coffee table and then said, "I came to take a little trip down memory lane. I haven't been this way in years."

Ellie's gaze softened, her expression one of understanding. "I see," she said, taking a sip from her glass.

I noticed a change in Ellie. The arrogance that had once radiated from her had softened to a quiet humility. Her eyes, once sparkling with mischievous intent, now reflected the wisdom born of years of life experiences and introspection. A pang of guilt surged through me, a feeling I quickly pushed aside.

"I often think about that summer," Ellie admitted at last. "When you and I first met."

I looked up, meeting Ellie's gaze. "So do I," I confessed. "More than I'd like to admit. I also think about everything that happened after that summer...with you and me...with Jack." I paused, taking a moment to collect my thoughts. "The truth is, Ellie ... I never should have done what I did. Especially not to you. As much as I wanted you to be the villain, to have deserved what I did, I was wrong. You were only doing what you had to do because you were in love with Jack, the same as me."

Ellie took a moment, letting my apology sink in. "I'm sorry, too," she said, "for not taking your feelings into consideration.

The way I acted when I came back for Clara's funeral was unacceptable, and if I could do it all over again..."

I gave a dismissive wave. "It isn't anything I wouldn't have done," I said, then laughed it off. "I just wish I could have seen earlier how foolish I was all those years, for chasing Jack around, hoping beyond hope that he would have a change of heart and love me the way he loved you. And for a time, I thought I had that. But in the back of my mind, I always knew he still had feelings for you, still hoped that you'd come back."

Ellie's eyes welled up with tears, and mine did the same. Finally, Ellie spoke, a distant look in her eyes. "I wish we could've understood each other better, back then. Perhaps things wouldn't have been so complicated, so fraught with hurt." She looked down at her glass, swirling the ice around as if it held some hidden answer. "And Jack...he suffered the most. He didn't deserve that."

"You're right..." I nodded, my gaze faraway. "Jack was stuck in the middle of our chaos, like a ship between two storms."

Ellie nodded, seeming to agree with my sentiment. She took a deep breath, then looked back up at me. "He loved us both, in his own way," she admitted. "I think he just didn't know how to handle it."

"I suppose none of us did," I replied, a sad smile playing on my lips.

In the seconds that followed, I realized something. We were no longer girls, but women carrying the weight of their own world's burdens.

After what felt like an eternity, Ellie placed her glass on the table and looked at me earnestly. "How different things might have been if we had made other choices."

I nodded, my gaze dropping to her half-empty glass. The

ice had begun to melt, diluting the sweet tea. I swirled my glass in my hand as I pondered Ellie's statement. "But we made the choices we thought were best at the time," I said, the words heavy in the quiet room. "And in the end, I'm satisfied with how things turned out."

Ellie gave a weak but understanding smile, nodding in agreement. A long silence stretched between us again, but this time it wasn't an uncomfortable one. It was more like a mutual understanding, a shared acknowledgment of the past we could not change, only learn from.

My eyes met Ellie's. Our reminiscing gaze held echoes of the past that still clung to us both. "I think it's time we moved on, don't you?"

She was silent at first, her eyes thoughtful as they continued to bore into mine. But then she nodded slowly.

"Yes," Ellie agreed softly, the single word holding so much weight. "Yes, it is." She raised her glass, the remaining liquid sloshing lightly against the edges.

I did the same, lifting my own glass. The clinking sound reverberated in the air around us, a symbol of something new, something hopeful. "To moving forward," I proposed.

"To moving forward."

We drank in unison, the sweet tea washing down our throats like a bitter-sweet memory. The sound of the glasses on the table seemed to echo the finality of our decision. It was time to move on, time to let go.

Suddenly, Ellie looked up at the clock, then back to me. "Did you want to see Jack? He should be home anytime now."

"No," I replied abruptly. I did not wish to see the man who had inadvertently caused so much turbulence in my life. It felt like opening an old wound, and I simply didn't have the strength to face him. "I mean, I would, but I need to be on my way."

Ellie nodded, understanding the implied boundaries. "It was good to see you, Sara," she said, standing up from her chair. The late afternoon sun was slanting through the lace curtains, casting a warm glow on her face and making her auburn hair shimmer. "And I mean that."

I, too, rose from my chair and nodded, extending my hand. "It was good to see you too, Ellie." Our hands met in a firm handshake, a final semblance of our shared past and the conclusion of a difficult conversation.

I moved toward the door, putting one foot in front of the other.

"He never forgot you," she said as I reached for the knob.

I took a step, stopped, and turned back to her. Our eyes locked, and I found myself lost in the depth of her gaze. For a moment, I allowed myself to imagine an alternate reality where things had taken a different turn. A reality where Jack and I were together, spared of the heartache I'd caused. But that wasn't our reality. We had chosen different paths, and this was where we ended up, back where we started.

I felt a pang at the thought of the what-ifs, the could-have-beens, but it quickly subsided as reality surfaced. "Neither did I," I admitted, my voice heavy with emotion.

Ellie gave me a warm smile, and just as I was leaving, whispered, "Take care, Sara." As I stepped out into the cool evening air, I felt a strange mixture of relief and sadness wash over me. I turned to Ellie, giving her one last look that said more than words ever could—thanks for understanding, sorry for everything, take care.

Walking away from that house felt a little like walking away from a ghost. It was an echo of my past in the most tangible sense. With each step, a weight lifted off my shoulders. Perhaps it was the final acknowledgement of what had happened, or the catharsis of my confession, but I felt a sense of closure I hadn't experienced before, like I had finally managed to put this whole nasty business behind me.

As I drove away, I glanced back one last time at the old house. For years, it had been a symbol of my mistakes. Now, it just seemed like an ordinary house, a monument to a time and place long gone. And as its silhouette receded into the deepening dusk, a chill ran down my spine, a shudder of finality that seemed to whisper in the wind—it's over now.

EPILOGUE

January 1994

"Here it is, as promised," said Diane, bursting into the library one afternoon with Cassie trailing behind her. "A couple of weeks later than I had hoped, but with the move and then the holidays..."

She handed me the manuscript, and I glanced at the title page—*A Thousand Distant Shores: The Life and Times of Sara Anne Hastings*.

"Read it at your leisure, of course" said Diane, throwing an arm around Cassie. "No rush. But when you get finished, let me know what you think."

"Thank you, dear. I think I'll start reading this now. So, where are you two off to?"

"Mom and I are going out for a walk," said Cassie. "She promised to take me to the beach today, so we could look for sand dollars."

"Oh, what fun," I said, smiling at the excitement in Cassie's eyes. "Come back later, and show me what treasures you've found. We can discuss it over a piece of that apple pie you like so much."

"Apple pie! Yay!" Cassie hopped up and down at the promise.

"All right, troublemaker," Diane said and kissed the top of

her head. "Let's go find those sand dollars."

And with that, they departed, leaving me alone with the manuscript. Judy wasn't due for another hour, so I settled into my favorite chair beside the fireplace, flipped open the cover, and started reading.

Introduction

They say that lighthouses are wise, steadfast, standing as beacons against the treacherous seas. But there is also a bit of loneliness about them, an isolation that is both necessary and melancholy.

Thirty minutes south of Kitty Hawk, North Carolina, stands the Bodie Island lighthouse, standing steadfast as it gazes out at the vastness of the restless Atlantic. In its shadow, the sand is strewn with relics of another age: rusty anchors, tattered ropes, and fragments of sun-bleached driftwood.

Beneath the lighthouse's watchful eye is where a heartbroken young woman once sought refuge, where she began a journey that would forever change the course of her life. And it is here, at the place where the sand meets the sea, that I reflect on this woman who has meant so much to so many, whose life story now rests within these pages.

Her name is Sara Anne Hastings. She is a wife, friend, judge, adventurer, and activist. Like the lighthouse she so admires, she has stood tall in the face of life's challenges, her wisdom serving as a guiding light for those lost in the stormy seas of life. Sara's journey began as the daughter of a seamstress and ended with her as one of the most revered judges in the state. Her life is a symbol of resilience and determination amidst chaos, a testament to the unbreakable human spirit that refuses to surrender to life's turbulent storms.

But Sara's story is not simply one of success and admiration. Hers is a deeply human tale, filled with both joy and sorrow, love and sacrifice. It started with a determined young girl who defied societal expectations and embraced the unknown that lay ahead. What came next was an awakening of sorts, a kind of rebirth from the ashes. For Sara, it was an opportunity for her to rediscover herself. Where she once followed in the shadows of others, she now stands confidently in her own light, forging her own path and writing her own story.

Heartbreak reshaped her, not into a bitter woman harboring resentments and regrets, but rather into a stronger woman who found strength in her vulnerabilities. She grew a backbone of steel, one that refused to break under the weight of sadness or disappointment. Her spirit remained undaunted; she laughed with unrestrained joy and loved with an open, generous heart, but she no longer threw herself into the whirlwind of infatuation with the reckless abandon of her youth. A wisdom had settled over her, a knowledge born from heartache and endurance that taught her to thread care with passion, to ensure prudence took precedence over blind love.

Even to this day, Sara's keen wisdom continues to steer

her in the right direction. Her legacy is not simply defined by her impactful rulings and the causes she has fought for, but also by the way she has shed light on those around her. Her impact can be compared to that of a lighthouse, radiating an otherworldly glow and providing guidance for lost souls looking for refuge during turbulent times. And just like the lighthouse that she loves so much, the one that overlooks this familiar stretch of ocean, when it comes to weathering the storm, Sara Hastings stands alone.

THE END

ACKNOWLEDGEMENTS

As always, I would like to thank the individuals who played key roles in shaping this story into what it is today.

To my agent, Katie Monson, thank you for your continued support. To Meredith Wild, Jordyn Wentworth, and the amazing team at Page & Vine, it has been an absolute pleasure working with you on this companion novel.

A special shoutout to my beta readers, Shania, Chloeey, Evelyn, and Brooke, for their time in scrutinizing this manuscript and helping make it the best it can be.

I must also thank my wife, Josette, for her patience and understanding as I revisited the world of Sara, Jack, and Ellie. None of this would be possible without your love and support.

And last but not least, to my readers, your unwavering support is what keeps me writing. You're the best!

ABOUT THE AUTHOR

Buck Turner is the bestselling author of seven novels, including *The Long Road Back to You, I'll Wait, The Hearts We Leave Behind,* and *Evergreen.* A former IT professional turned writer, he lives with his family in Northern Kentucky.

ALSO BY BUCK TURNER